How to START
Your Own
BUSINESS

How to START Your Own BUSINESS

by Henry G. Solomon

Small Business Assistance of America
A Division of Solomon BDI, Inc.

How to **Start Your Own Business**

Copyright © 2015

by Henry G. Solomon

Cover by: Penny Williams

ISBN: 978-0-692-36808-4

www.SmallBusinessAA.com

Email: Info@SmallBusinessAA.com

Printed in U.S.A

DEDICATION

I thank God for the support I have from family and friends.

To my Dad for teaching me the value of dedication and hard work.

To my Mom for always being there for me.

To Sophie for showing me the value of family.

To Mike for helping me stay focused and grounded.

To my son for making life worthwhile.

To Penny for being the most dedicated and committed person I've ever known.

To Rob for your hard work, advice, and encouragement.

To Linda for your prayers and amazing faith.

To Larry for your strength, always being there for me and for being the wisest person I've ever known. It was an honor to have known you. You will be extremely missed and never forgotten 1952-2015.

How to Start Your Own Business

A WORD TO THOSE STARTING A BUSINESS

Starting a new business can be incredibly exciting and extremely nerve-racking. You are the boss; you have to make the tough choices, and you make the biggest paycheck of all your employees. The purpose of this book is to give you insight, options, and explanations with regard to starting a small business. The life of a business owner can be tremendously rewarding and at the same time intensely challenging. How you handle the situations you face will determine a step forward or a step backwards.

This book provides you with step-by-step instruction, in-depth information, knowledge, guidance, and advice on the topics listed in the chapters' section.

This book is written direct and easy to understand. There are several interactive sections in this book where the reader will answer questions or make business decisions.

When starting a new business, one thing you must understand is that success is not going to just magically fall out of the sky and end up on your lap. You have to get up, straighten up, and get a plan; stay focused, stay determined, and most of all never give up. Will there be fears, doubts, and hardships? Of course but how you handle them will determine the outcome.

The only thing standing between you and your goals are the steps it takes to get there. You can do anything you put your mind and heart into, but not everything is profitable.

Do you have a passion about your business idea? I hope so, because you will need it.

Passion alone does not equal a successful business. You need to understand your business industry inside and out and have a realistic and strategic business plan combined with the ability to execute it.

If you are lazy, lack goal motivation, want the success of life to come to you freely with no hard work, long hours, sweat, or tears, and you *are not* willing to change; this book is not for you!

If you are goal motivated, ready to move forward, willing to put in hard work to see your dreams turn into an actual reality, then this book is definitely for you!

Let's take these steps together.

"The only thing standing between you and your goals

are the steps it takes to get there."

 *In addition to this book, we offer other services that help you get your business up and running. Please visit our website at www.SmallBusinessAA.com for more information.*

THINGS TO KNOW BEFORE STARTING

1. There are no guarantees of success in business. All business involves some sort of risk. If you want a guarantee of success, this book is not for you.

2. This is not a get rich quick by doing "no hard work" instructional handbook.

3. This is not a "recruit three to five people under you and make commissions" instructional handbook.

4. Expect to be challenged and instructed step by step to achieve your goals.

5. Expect to do a lot of hard work and essential planning, combined with strategic thinking.

6. Expect to make business decisions.

7. Expect to receive abundant and valuable information from this book.

8. You will receive advice and instruction but the choice to accept is yours to make.

9. Your success depends on the choices you make.

A small business is defined as one that is independently owned and operated, is organized for profit, and is not dominant in its field. The business may have up to 1500 employees and generate revenues not to exceed $21.5 million depending upon the industry and size eligibility. (SBA)

Conventions Used In This Book

 A Bit of Knowledge that can be helpful in your business.

 Author Experience: Personal situations and events that were experienced by the author.

 Goals: Realistic achievable goals.

 Important: Important information that may be valuable in your business.

 Interactive: Sections requiring your input to evaluate your position and guide you toward making sound decisions concerning your business.

 Note: Important things to remember and apply to your business.

 Small Business Assistance of America additional services.

 Smart Idea: Ideas or hints that may benefit you and your business.

 Smart Tips: Informative tips that can benefit you in your business.

 Sound Wisdom: Knowledge and advice that are priceless in your business.

PREFACE

"A Note from the Author"

My top three words to consider when starting a new business are:

FOCUS · DETERMINATION · CHANGE

- Stay focused on the task at hand and strive to achieve your short-term goals.

- Be determined: do not give up because of obstacles.

- Do not be afraid of change: change is a good thing when it brings forth progress.

Here are some characteristics of the most successful people in the world.

- It is likely their day begins before the sun rises.

- Their day was already planned at least a day or weeks beforehand.

- Their days are planned with reaching goals in mind.

- The doubts of others do not sway them.

- Staying focused is a major priority.

- Goals reached are celebrated for a brief time and then they are met with new and more challenging goals to attain.

- They keep pushing and moving forward.

- Failure is an opportunity to change, adjust, and learn how *not to do* something.

"I've not failed. I've just found 10,000 ways that won't work." (Edison)

Table of Contents

Chapter 1

Chapter 2

Chapter 3

Chapter 4

Chapter 5

Chapter 6

Understanding Your Business: *"Make Sure You Know Your Business Inside & Out"* _____ 57

Chapter 7

Be Aware of Critics and Negative People: *"A Successful Person Can be Certain of this; There will Never be a Shortage of Critics"* _____ 79

Chapter 11

Chapter 12

Chapter 13

Chapter 14

Chapter 15

Chapter 16

Chapter 20

Chapter 21

Chapter 22

Focus on Providing an Excellent Product and Customer Service:

Chapter 23

Sales & Negotiating: *"Every Business Should do their Best to Save Money, Keep Costs Low, and Sell their Products or Services at a Fair and Reasonable Price which in Turn, Will Produce a Profit."*

Chapter 24

Maximizing Your Business Potential: *"They are already Your Customers; Increase Customer Satisfaction and Sales by Offering them Additional Products or Services."*

Chapter 30

Chapter 31

Chapter 32

Chapter 33

Chapter 34

Bibliography

INTRODUCTION

Our desire at Small Business Assistance of America is for you to be successful in your business endeavors. We believe the contents of this instructional handbook will help you with that success.

The best way to start a business is by keeping expenses as low as possible. With that in mind, we have several cost effective services to assist you when starting your business.

In this book, you will find some information repeated in different chapters. It is done on purpose to stress how important it is and relevant to the chapter you are reading.

There are many diverse industries and various business types within those industries therefore, this book is written as generic as possible for you. Within the chapters, we use a few business examples so you only need to apply the advice to your specific business if appropriate.

Once you purchase our instructional handbook, consider yourself part of the Small Business Assistance of America family. Make sure to register your email address on our website to ensure that you receive periodic updates, tips, advice, access to new product releases and exclusive content.

Now, find a quiet secluded environment, take a deep breath, clear your mind, and learn *"How to Start Your Own Small Business."*

Thank you,

Henry G. Solomon
Author - Small Business Consultant
Small Business Assistance of America

*Visit www.SmallBusinessAA.com for a complete list of available services.

Chapter 1

Quick Start-Up Guide

"Most people start businesses based on their

knowledge, passion, and experience."

This chapter is directed to those who want to get a jump-start in their new business, which is perfectly OK, just proceed cautiously. I will go through the basics here, but strongly suggest you read the entire book before officially venturing out. If you wish to take a more thorough approach, start with Chapter 2.

Step 1: Business Idea, Passion, Knowledge, Experience & Funding

List your business idea(s).

_____

_____

_____

_____

Determine which business idea(s) you are the most passionate about.

If you only have one business idea, on a scale from 1-10 how passionate are you about it?

_____

_____

Now list the business idea(s) you are the most knowledgeable about.

If you only have one business idea on a scale from 1-10 how knowledgeable are you about it?

_____

_____

How many years of experience do you have in the business type(s) you want to start?

_____

_____

_____

List the business idea that you can start based on the amount of capital (available cash) you have on hand.

_____

_____

_____

If you do not have capital to invest, do you have collateral to get a business loan?

Yes   or   No   Circle your answer.

The standard amount of collateral is 20% of the loan amount.

If yes, then list your collateral type.

_____

Let's go over your answers.

Consider your business ideas, passion, knowledge, experience, and capital or collateral amounts. Which business idea do you feel is the best option?

_____

_____

Step 2: Industry, Location, Hours, Products & Pricing

What is your business industry and type? Example: Fashion industry, online clothing and accessory store.

_____

Does your business sell to consumers, businesses, or both?

_____

Will you operate from a physical location or home and why?

_____

What days and hours are you able to operate your business?

_____

Is your business seasonal or year round?

_____

If seasonal, which months of the year will you be open for business?

_____

If year round, which months of the year do you anticipate the greatest amount of sales?

_____

Tip: Save or invest during peak seasons to help you get through slower seasons.

What products or services will you offer?

_____

_____

_____

_____

How much will you sell them for?

_____

_____

_____

_____

How much does your competition sell them for?

_____

_____

_____

_____

Choosing to sell your products less expensive than your competition is good, however, remember cheaper is not always better. To a number of people cheaper means exactly that, "You get what you pay for!" Depending on your customer base, they may expect some items to cost a certain amount, which would depict quality and value. So study your customer base and products before deciding prices.

Step 3: Business Registration & Website Development

Read Chapter 8 for assistance on choosing an entity type.

List a few business names. In the event your first choice is not available for registration, you will have a few more options to select from.

_____

_____

Which business names are easy to spell and remember? This is important when your customers are trying to find you on the Internet.

_____

_____

_____

_____

Choose one business name:

_____

Permits and licensing differ depending on industry and business type. You will need to determine which permits or licenses are required to operate your business. (See Chapter 10, "Sales Tax, EIN, Licensing and Permits for more information on permits and licenses.)

Once your business name has been registered you will need to determine the set of colors your business will use and decide on a logo and slogan for your business.

Next you should have a professional and responsive website developed. A responsive website means customers can view your website on a desktop computer screen, laptop, tablet, or mobile device. Your website should also have the same look and feel of your business cards, brochures, etc.

 Visit SmallBusinessAA.com for more information concerning Business Registration, Website Development & Online Store, Domain Name (website name), Business Email, Credit Card Processing, Graphic Design & Advertising Materials.

Step 4: Advertising, Hiring & Company Policies

(This subject is explained in more detail under Chapter 21, "Advertising & Marketing.")

- Determine who your target market is.
- List details concerning customers who are most likely to purchase your products.

Example: Age group, male or female, income levels, single, couples, families, etc.

Gather as much information as possible as this will help you determine which advertisements to choose and how to present your ads.

_____

_____

_____

_____

Start placing ads at least one month before you launch your business. Add a **"Coming Soon"** label to build anticipation.

When placing advertisements make sure they are geared towards your target market, that they are located within an area your potential customers are and through a source your potential customers are most likely to use.

What source will you advertise your business through? Ideas may include the Internet, billboards, commercials, flyers, local papers, magazines, etc.)

_____

_____

Make sure to negotiate pricing and terms.

Every company should have a set of company policies they abide by.

Write down your company policies, and include your refund policy.

_____

_____

_____

_____

_____

_____

_____

_____

_____

_____

Write down the policies you want your employees to follow (if applicable).

_____

_____

_____

_____

Step 5: Planning and Strategies

Be certain you write a specific plan covering all aspects and details concerning your business. Describe exactly what you want to do and define how you will proceed to implement it. Stepping out without a plan is a recipe for failure.

Answer these questions:

What do you want to do?

_____

_____

_____

What steps will it take to accomplish this?

_____

_____

_____

How long will it take? _____

Give yourself a deadline date for projects so you will stay on task. During the preparation phase, days off are very limited. Use a calendar and write details of what needs to be done and by when. Stay focused on completing daily goals. Decide how and where you will get your products, and determine ways to deliver quality not just quantity when servicing your customers. Have a plan B, C, D, and E available in case your first plans do not work out. Once you have a plan and strategy in place, try to find other ways you can accomplish it more efficiently and for less cost.

Have a plan in place detailing what you will do with the profits you make. Take in account, future expenses before spending any profits. As a new business, your plan must include the months of the year sales will be higher, moderate, and lower and adjust your budgets for those times. Depending on your business type, seasons of the year may play a factor in your sales. For example, summer time means real estate agents, movers, tour and travel agencies, etc. are very busy. Wintertime means stores are full of shoppers eager to buy the perfect gift.

Step 6: Sales & Profits

Make sure your sales price is competitive and able to produce profits for your company. If your expenses outweigh your sales, you will be losing money. Come up with a sales pitch and strategy. How will you approach your customers and why they should purchase from you instead of a competing business?

_____

_____

_____

One hardship new businesses face is the undeniable fact that they are a "new" business. There is no established trust in your business or the quality of your products or services. You will have to build that trust by exhibiting excellent customer service, knowledge and experience in your business type. Let your customers know they are valued, respected, and appreciated. Not only with words but with actions.

During your first months of business you may consider giving higher discounts than you normally would. First time customers will appreciate the discount but turning them into repeat customers will depend on sales prices, convenience, and customer service. You are the new business on the block, so people will be curious but curiosity does not equal sales. Delivering excellent products and exceptional customer service does.

What else can you offer your customers? Aside from your products or services, are there other items that you can provide that will interest your customers? Example: Gas stations have convenience stores. If you own a music store, you could offer music lessons. If you own an electronic store, you may want to offer technical support.

_____

_____

_____

What forms of payment will you accept?

_____

Visit SmallBusinessAA.com for more information concerning Business Registration, Website Development & Online Store, Domain Name (website name), Business Email, Credit Card Processing, Graphic Design & Advertising Materials.

Step 7: Taxes, Expenses, & Insurance

My best advice on this subject (Taxes & Expenses) is to hire an accountant on a monthly basis once you start making progressive sales. They have professional experience in this field and the monthly cost saves you time that you can spend on sales or marketing. (For more details see Chapter Titled, "Taxes, Expenses and Business Insurance.)

Purchasing products, rental fees, equipment, phone systems, advertising costs, etc. are considered business expenses. They will be deducted from your total sales amount so you will not be taxed on your total sales but rather your total sales minus business expenses.

Make sure you do countless research to determine if there are better ways to acquire products less expensive and quicker. I suggest every year researching to discover if you can save money on your expenses. If you find a lower cost, convey the amount to your current supplier, they may match the cost to keep your business. Keep in mind that when you decide to buy from another vendor, that cheaper is not always better.

Once I switched suppliers, only to find out that the products took two extra weeks and were poor in quality. The wait time and poor quality was not worth the few dollars saved. Lesson learned.

Every business should at minimum have a general liability insurance policy. Business type and location are just a couple of factors to help determine the amount of coverage you need and if you need additional policies. Whether you operate out of your home, retail, or office insurance is necessary to protect you, your investment, and your company. Do not launch your company without proper insurance first.

Step 8: Launch Day!

Time to put your preparation to the test! *Launch with confidence!* By this time, you should be ready to get started. Will it be perfect? No way! Will there be needed adjustments? Absolutely! Do not wait until everything is perfect because "perfect" may never come. You will be nervous and feel anxious but take a deep breath and welcome to the world of *entrepreneurship*.

You may find in the first days of operation that you get more inquiries instead of sales. Make sure you leave any potential customer with a good lasting impression; one that they will remember and tell their friends. Make sure you give out business cards, brochures, and direct them to your website, and be excited about your products or services! Your excitement will be passed on to your employees and customers!

> *Launch with confidence!*

READY · SET · SALES!

You have just completed the Quick Start-up Guide.

Our goal at Small Business Assistance of America is to help you get your business up and running while keeping costs low as possible. We believe in you and will assist you every step of the way. We offer other services on our website to assist you with starting your new business.

Visit www.SmallBusinessAA.com for help with:

- Registering your business.

- Registering your domain name (business name registered on the Internet).

- Registering your business email.

- Developing your website and e-commerce store.

- Assist in setting-up your business to accept credit cards.

- Graphic design and advertising materials.

- And more!

Chapter 2

Believe You Can Succeed

"Don't Fear Failure, Fear Never Trying."

Believing you can succeed is one of the most important things you can do. Without believing you can succeed, you will be filled with doubts, second-guessing yourself, and will not have enough confidence in your products or services.

Will you have doubts? Of course, you will.

Will there be fear and anxiety? Most definitely, you can count on it. The solution is not giving into those doubts, fears, and anxiety. Instead, let the confidence of knowing you can succeed outweigh them.

> *"An idea is just an idea unless you do what is necessary to turn your idea into a reality."*

What is Success?

Please, let me explain something that I believe personally. Success is not just about making money (although it is a significant part). It is about loving what you do, it is about fulfillment of joy and happiness while conquering the challenges of life. Success is reaching the goals you have set for yourself, not the goals others think you should achieve. I have seen miserable millionaires and joyful janitors.

Consider the Successful Examples around You.

Take a moment and think about the successful businesses that operate in your area. Consider national chain stores or mom and pop local businesses. Before they stepped out and decided to start a business, it was just an idea, a thought, a desire to provide a product or service that would fulfill a need or solve a problem. They were confident in their ideas, filled with the belief that if they took the right steps, they could one day turn those ideas into reality.

Only you can determine if you have the faith and confidence to believe you can succeed. No one else can determine that for you. Once you believe you can, there are steps that are necessary to prepare you for business ownership. After completion of these steps, you will be able to execute them. The results of your idea, preparation and execution become sales.

"You will never achieve what you first cannot see in your mind"

Confidence = Idea + Preparation + Execution

Idea + Preparation + Execution = Sales

- Confidence helps produce ideas.

- Confidence gives you the push you need to take actual steps in preparing for your business.

- Confidence helps execute your business plans.

How many times have people exclaimed they "want to" or "someday" will start a business? Lack of confidence will push their "want to" and "someday" to "never".

Your business idea should be something that you are great at. It should be something that you have passion, considerable knowledge and experience in. Preparation should begin well in advance of your expected start date. Launch day is when you execute all of your hard work. Sales will soon follow.

Neither preparation nor execution is possible without the confidence in believing your idea will succeed.

Do you believe you can succeed?

Speak it → See it → Believe it → Walk in it

<u>**Speak**</u> out loud that you will succeed in your goals.

Take time to day dream and <u>***see it***</u> in your mind.

Eventually your heart will <u>***believe it***</u> as well.

Next, take the necessary steps to <u>***walk in it***</u>.

Whether you are starting a new business or have been in business for some time, you will be faced with challenges and doubts. I need you to understand that your circumstances or past failures do not define you. You are a fighter, you are able to stand up, get focused, get a plan, and walk towards what you believe success is for your life.

Will starting or operating your business be easy? No, if it were easy then everyone would do it. However, with appropriate preparation, determination, focus, and a well thought out strategic plan it will all be worth it when you live out your dreams.

"See it in your mind then make it a reality in your life."

Final Advice

> *"You Only Fail If You Stop Trying"*

Your first business may or may not be what you do for the rest of your life. People start businesses, operate them for years, and pass them down to their children. Some people start businesses, sell them, and start new ones. You have to find out which business works for you. If your first idea works great, that is a huge plus. If it does not, do not think selling or closing a business as a failure. Think of it as a step in another direction.

On a Personal Note,

Rarely in life is anyone perfect at all things. We all must learn not to be too hard on ourselves because of past mistakes. In fact, since you are reading this book, it proves that you are willing to take positive steps. Are you going to have doubts and fears? Of course, you will. Every business owner deals with that, myself included. The difference is not giving in to those uncertainties.

"You Only Fail If You Stop Trying!"

"Stay positive, believe you can succeed, take the necessary steps, and move forward."

Chapter 3

Develop a Positive Mindset

"Do your best to keep a positive mindset so you can recognize the existing opportunities that are right in front of you."

T he only thing standing in the way of your goals becoming a reality are the steps it takes to get there. Are you willing to take positive steps towards your goals?

Someone may see just an old house while someone else perceives an opportunity.

Yes   or   No   (Circle one)

"Doubts And Lack Of Confidence Can Be Your Biggest Enemy"

As we grow up, we learn to think a certain way, act a certain way, and are taught how to view things. Your upbringing will sometimes determine your outlook, and it can be negative or positive.

Think BIG, Think Opportunity

As an entrepreneur, it is important that you learn to see opportunities in front of you. Someone may see just an old house while someone else perceives an opportunity. A chance to buy cheap, repair, paint, furnish, and sell for a profit.

Many people think come to work, clock in, lunchtime, clock out, and go home. Make an hourly wage, pay the bills, and occasionally take a vacation, and they are happy. Some people work for a company for many years and then retire. For those who choose to do that, it is perfectly OK. There is nothing wrong with that lifestyle as long as they are happy in their position.

"If everyone chose to own a business,

there wouldn't be any employees to help run them."

The fact that you are reading this book proves that you want to be a business owner and not an employee. Many people, including me were told many times that they were failures and will never be anything in life. Unfortunately, some people actually begin to believe this and lose all motivation to move forward with their dreams.

Discover Your Mindset

"It is not what others think, it is what you believe that matters."

Answer the questions below as honestly as possible. They may seem somewhat personal but will give you an idea of where you are mentally. Having a positive attitude is so important while operating your business.

 How do you see things? – Bright and filled with opportunity, dark and negative, or somewhere in the middle?

_____

What business opportunities are available to you right now?

_____

Why have you waited to seize these opportunities? Lack of knowledge, confidence, fears, money, know-how, or something else?

_____

Do you view situations for what they are or for what they can be?

_____

Do you need the validation or approval of others in order to do something new?

_____

Are you able to succeed despite what anyone tells you?

_____

When you see an opportunity, do you think it will be too difficult, do you see it as a challenge you can conquer, or somewhere in the middle?

_____

If too difficult, explain why?

_____

_____

_____

If you can conquer, explain why?

_____

_____

_____

If somewhere in the middle, explain why?

_____

_____

_____

Your answers show where your mindset is. Only you can determine if you are satisfied with the results or need to make a few changes.

Opportunities are all around us. Some people wait until one is presented and some people make their own. We can choose to act or let it pass us by.

List Your Strengths

List your top five strengths as they pertain to business (administration, customer service oriented, planning and strategy, business operations, creative, marketing, etc).

_____

_____

_____

_____

_____

"Opportunities are all around us. Some people wait until one is presented and some people make their own. We can choose to act or let it pass us by."

When operating your business, make sure you are operating within your strengths. Do not try to excel at something in which you do not possess sufficient skills. Hire employees for positions where you lack excellence. One trait of successful entrepreneurs is placing employees in their appropriate positions according to their strengths.

Learn from Your Past Mistakes and Failures, and Then Let them Go!

The next lists pertain to business or life in general.

INTERACTIVE

Think about your past mistakes and failures and write what you have learned from them?

_____

_____

_____

_____

_____

_____

Once you have learned from your past failures, let them go. Take full opportunity of the present and believe for a bright and better future. It is extremely important to have a positive attitude and mindset before starting a business.

Remember your past victories and successes often!

If you are going to spend time thinking about the past, remember the times where you had success and victory instead of defeat. Choose to think positive.

 List your past victories and successes and write what you have learned from them?

_____

_____

_____

_____

_____

_____

Tips to Help Think Positive

The definition of positive is to be confident in opinion and have no possibility of doubt. (Dictionary)

The act of thinking positive or having a positive attitude is a work-in-progress and will be something to work towards. The focus is for you to get the past behind you and press on to a brighter and better future. This is something I personally had to do and still do, to maintain a positive outlook. Letting your past failures go and working towards a positive attitude and mindset are priceless! The benefits will help you not just in business but also in everyday life.

> *"Let go of your past failures and mistakes, but before you do, learn from them."*

Here are some tips:

 *Tip 1: Speak Positive on Purpose*

This may seem silly at first for some, yet, the more you speak aloud the greater is the chance your mind will believe it. Once your mind believes it, you will start to believe it in your heart as well. You have to be able to see yourself successful in your mind before you are successful in reality.

Start speaking positive things aloud to yourself about your success. You are a person that can succeed in whatever you put your mind, heart, and strength into. Verbally say that you have let go of your past mistakes, failures, and choose to have a positive mindset and attitude.

Here is an example of speaking aloud, positively.

Example: I am a successful business owner because I have what it takes to be successful. I am smart; I am wise; I make good business decisions; and I am positioning myself for success.

I have learned from my past failures and let them go. I will move forward with my life in a positive direction. I am able to apply what I have learned and make positive decisions in my life and business. I am more than able to take the necessary steps to reach my goals.

Tip 2: Focus on Accomplishing Attainable Short Term Goals

Set goals with a time frame and work towards them.

Write down some short-term goals with dates and continue to read them aloud daily.

I will achieve the goal of _____

by _____ (write date).

I will achieve the goal of _____

by _____ (write date).

I will achieve the goal of _____

by _____ (write date).

Setting goals without giving yourself a time frame can cause you to lose focus and persistence.

Write the steps it will take to achieve each goal here.

Goal 1

_____

_____

_____

Goal 2

_____

_____

_____

Goal 3

_____

_____

_____

 *Tip 3: Never Stop Learning*

We live in a fast-paced world with endless information at our fingertips. Take advantage of the opportunity to learn more about your industry and other areas of your business. There are books, eBooks, and videos on just about every aspect of any business. You can find information produced by people who have been in business for years and share their knowledge. There are business magazines you can subscribe to that will interview some of the richest people in the world who give insight to their success. Secrets of success are not secrets anymore, just look them up online.

 Tip 4: Be Inspired By the Success of Others

Begin reading about other successful people and discover how they first started. Learn about how they made mistakes and failed a few times but never gave up. There are endless amounts of success stories, and I encourage you to research and read them.

"Not everyone starts out on top; many times success is a journey and not a quick ride."

"*Position yourself to succeed*"

 *On a Personal Note,*

Thinking positive is a state of mind that develops over time. No one can think positive all the time. You will have doubts, fears or uneasiness. It is normal to feel that way when doing something brand new. The difference is how you respond to it.

Moving forward in life or business is a great indication that you are on the right track and are ready to conquer new challenges that await you. If you learned negativity from your surroundings and came to believe that negativity for a long time, it may take longer to change your mindset. I encourage you to make "developing a positive mindset" an everyday practice in your daily life and the life of your loved ones.

Words are very powerful and can have a lasting impact on you and those who are most important to you. You are able to do everything that is in your heart to do. With instruction, guidance, encouragement, and an opportunity — nothing can stop you!

A positive mindset empowers you to progress; progression enables you to make a difference in your life and the lives of others.

Chapter 4

Business Tips and Advice

"Every business exists to deliver a solution to a problem."

A Few Ingredients That Lead To a Successful Business.

- Provide solutions to problems.

- Charge an affordable price (according to its target market) that can compete when compared to your competition.

- Your goal is to make your monthly total sales much higher than your monthly expenses.

- Be able to communicate effectively to your actual and potential customers, in person and through advertisements.

- Provide exceptional customer service.

- Be available during the times your customers are most likely to purchase from you.

- Have more than one purchasing option (In person, over the phone, online, etc.).

- Be willing to go above and beyond to deliver a product or service that exceeds your customers' expectations.

- Know your competition.

- Be ready to handle customer service issues and refunds.

- Make sure to over staff during busy times and peak seasons.

- Be passionate about your business.

- Have a strategic, realistic, and attainable business plan.

- Stay on budget.

- Location, location, location!

- Ask for customer referrals.

Tip 1: Be a Problem Solver

Every business in the world exists to deliver solutions to problems, through either products, services or both for a person, group, or another company.

- If you are hungry, there are grocery stores, restaurants, cafés etc.

- If you need directions, there are printed maps, GPS products, or navigational apps on your smart phone.

- If you are thirsty, there are water fountains, water bottles, and water faucets.

- If you need to travel from one place to another there are cars, planes, trains, subways, bicycles, etc.

Someone at some point started a business, which made those products or services available for use. Ensure you outline the problems your business solves and how it solves them.

 Tip 2: Always Offer Fair Prices According to Your Target Market

When determining the price you will charge for your products or services, make sure you do extensive research beforehand. Know the current market rate other businesses are charging that sell to similar target markets. For instance, a clothing store in a neighborhood whose homes sell for $500K or more will most likely charge more for their products than a clothing store in a neighborhood whose homes sell for $100K or less.

If the cost for your products is too high, your potential customers cannot afford it. If the cost is especially low, your prospective customers may not have faith in the value of your products or services. Be sure you are charging fair rates according to your target market.

Tip 3: Your Sales Should be Much Higher than Your Monthly Expenses

The goal for every business is to make profits from their sales. In order to accomplish this every business must take into account the cost to purchase products, advertising expenses, time spent providing services, etc. The list of costs depends on your business type. Make sure that you spend a significant amount of time figuring out ways to cut costs yet still deliver an excellent product or service. Doing so will increase your bottom line thus increase your profits.

Tip 4: Communicate to Your Target Market on a Level they Can Relate to

Your business must be able to communicate effectively to your target market. A detailed explanation of this tip is in Chapter 21 titled, "Advertising & Marketing."

Tip 5: Treat Your Customers, as You Would Want to be Treated

Excellent customer service is one of the main aspects to running a successful business. Staff your customer service department with outstanding performers. No one likes to speak with a customer service rep who is disrespectful or uninformed. Make sure your team is well trained and qualified to handle customer service issues with excellence. Remember, long lasting businesses are built by satisfying one customer at a time.

Tip 6: Hours of Operation and Customer Availability

Ensure your hours of operation are the hours your customers are able to purchase from you. Even if you run a website, which can handle sales 24 hours a day, you still need to have a customer-service phone number for inquiries. Do not make

35

the mistake and be an "email only" business. That method of communication, as a small business, can cost you tons of lost sales.

 Tip 7: Have More than One Purchasing Option

It is important to provide your customers with several purchasing options. Some customers prefer in person, while others prefer over the phone or online, etc. Having several purchasing options available will provide your customers convenient access to purchase your products or services.

Purchasing options could include but are not limited to:

In person, over the phone, online through your website, faxing in an order along with credit card details, through an email link which directs to your website for purchasing, a smart phone app which allows purchasing, and sending a check through the mail.

 Tip 8: Going Above and Beyond Your Customers' Expectations

This will have your customers bragging about your business to their family and friends and will win their loyalty. Be careful though because they will expect that level of service every time so make sure to stay consistent.

 Tip 9: Know Your Competition

Some of your competitors would love to take your customers from you. As much as we want to think we live in a fair world, we do not. Some of your competition is out to beat your sales prices, take your customers, and close your doors.

Do not focus on your competition but do not be oblivious of them either. Make sure your customer service is always improving and your prices are competitive. Always ask yourself this question. Why should customers purchase from me instead of my competitors? Your answer will provide you with what to focus on and always improve.

Some competing businesses may try to copy your ideas and business strategies. Do not make the mistake of over-thinking the situation. Doing so could cause you to lose focus on your main goals and cause you anger or frustration.

My advice (based on experience) is to not let your frustration or anger last too long. I do not believe there is a way to avoid feeling upset, but it does not have to consume your thought process. Make a decision to let it go and get over it. Learn to ignore these nuisances and return your focus to running and growing your business. If you let these emotions hang in there too long, it may soon control you.

 *Note: If you believe someone has stolen copy written work, trademark, or a patent of yours, consult an attorney.*

 ## *Tip 10: Be Ready to Handle Customer Service Issues and Refunds*

No matter how hard we try to deliver the best products and services, there will always be some customer-related issues. When dealing with the public or other businesses, ensure you have a process in place to handle those issues and keep your customers happy.

The term "the customer is always right" is not always true, however, one angry customer can cause more frustration than it is worth. I have refunded transactions merely on the fact that the actual cost of the product returned was less expensive, than the cost of the time it would take me to resolve the issue.

Setting up your own standards and policies and having customers read, sign, or click agree will help with the process of determining which action to take. Remember to determine if it is really worth the hassle or simply easier to refund and move on.

 Tip 11: Over Staff During Busy Hours and Peak Seasons

Over-staffing during busy hours and peak seasons is one effective way to deliver excellent customer service. You are able to ensure that your customers are handled in a timely manner and a happy customer is a repeat customer.

Let's admit it, no one likes to wait, not even you. Today, we live in a fast-paced society, and this can cause some customers to choose one business over the other simply based on wait time alone.

 Tip 12: Be Passionate About Your Products and/or Services

Your passion and excitement will be on display for others to see, and hopefully it will be contagious. We are most knowledgeable about our passions and continually strive for excellence when presenting them to others. Hire employees who are also passionate about the position they hold and you will reap the benefits of high customer satisfaction.

 Tip 13: Every Business Owner Needs A Business Plan

Make certain your plan is realistic with gradual growth. Set goals and write the steps it will take to achieve those goals. Let your plan include strategies for start-up, sustainability, growth, and longevity. Have a plan B, C, D, and E, in the event plan A does not work as expected.

An idea is just an idea unless you do what is necessary to turn your idea into a reality.

Tip 14: Have a Budget For Every Expense in Your Business

Know what every expense will cost you months in advance so you can prepare for it. Budgeting correctly will ensure that you do not spend profits without considering future expenses. Think about the bottom line when it comes to your profits. No matter how much you make in sales, it is the after expenses and taxes amount that will be what you have left at the end of every year.

 Tip 15: Location, Location, Location

Be accessible to your customers. Provide them with a convenient location to conduct business with you. Do not choose a location that is too hidden or so difficult to reach, that your customers will have to call you more than once for directions. If you are an online business, make sure your customers can communicate with you over the phone and through email or chats.

 Tip 16: Customer Referrals, an Entrepreneur's Best Friend

There is always a chance that your customer knows someone else that could benefit from your products or services. Never miss an opportunity to ask your satisfied customers for referrals.

Advice, Encouragement, Knowledge, and Wisdom

"Live everyday on purpose by accomplishing goals"

I have written several statements, advice, and business tips, which are not in any specific order. My goal is for you to learn from them and apply the encouragement, knowledge, and wisdom to your business decisions.

- A successful life is achieved in steps. So take good ones.

- Every day, you have a choice to either make good or bad decisions. Where you are in life right now is a product of the decisions you made in the past. The decisions you make now can determine where you will be in the future.

- On my calendar, I keep a list of short-term goals that I work towards on a daily basis (Mon-Fri).

- Grow your business gradually or find an investor instead of applying for a huge loan and placing your business into debt.

- The best type of business to start is something you actually possess passion, knowledge and experience in. In doing so, going to work will feel like no work at all. You will be able to enjoy what you do on a day-to-day basis. Although, keep in mind that passion, knowledge, and experience alone is not enough, you will need to focus on a realistic and attainable business plan combined with the ability to execute it.

- I view failure as an opportunity to learn "how not to" do something.

- At least, every three months take a step back and look at the big picture. Is your business where you want it to be? If not, ask yourself why and what can you do to change it? If yes, ask yourself what you can do to increase it?

- Strive towards excellence. Never be satisfied with your current situation. Slow yet progressive growth is better than no growth.

- Surround yourself with positive people.

- People usually adapt to the culture, conversations, and mannerisms of the group of people that surrounds them the most.

- It is easy for people to criticize your mistakes while staying in their comfort zone. At least, you are willing to try.

- Remember your victories and the hard times as well as what you did to overcome them in the past. You may not be where you should be, but at least you are not where you used to be. Hard times make you a stronger person.

- Never give up. Do not be afraid of change. Stay focused. Always move forward.

- Knowledge is not power! What you do with that knowledge is the power. You can have all the knowledge in the world, but if you do not put it to use, you will never know what you can achieve.

In the beginning stages of developing your business, focus on your **business processes** before immediate expansion.

Business Process— making sure your operations are flowing properly, your costs are low and your advertising and sales methods are working before deciding to grow, expand, or open more locations.

- **Grow**– add more products to your sales lists.

- **Expand**– add more office or warehouse space to your existing operations.

- **Open More Locations**– establishing multiple business units.

Do not mistake what I am saying and wait for your business process to be perfect. Perfection is rare; waiting for everything to be perfect could be a huge mistake. In business, you need to always be evolving and coming up with new, better, and less expensive ways to operate. Waiting too long to grow, expand, or open more locations could give your competition the upper hand.

"You only fail if you give up on your dreams."

Your "want to" has to be greater than the challenges you will face. A lot of people say "I want to _____" but rarely ever achieve it because of the challenges they face.

There are three kinds of people in this world. Those who make things happen. Those who talk about things that are happening. Those who exclaim, *"What happened?"* (Backley)

The fact that you are reading this book tells me you are in the category that makes things happen.

Be determined, focused, and well prepared.

Do not let the doubts of others influence you to the point of quitting, instead use their doubt as fuel to reach your goals.

No one will care more about your business than you.

You are the decision maker; you are the one who will wake up the earliest, arrive to work first and probably leave last (at least in the beginning stages).

Never put business before family.

No one on their deathbed ever said, "I wish I would have worked more" so do not forget to spend time with the ones who truly matter in life.

Do not wait until Monday to start something new! Start now! Get ahead!

Many people say, "I'll start on Monday," or "I'll start at the beginning of the month," or "I'll start next year." Often something comes up and there is a reason (excuse) that it does not happen on the stated start date. I chose to set a rule in my life and never start anything on a "Monday" but to start as soon as possible.

 *No one is perfect.*

Rules, guidelines, and plans are great to live by and stick to, but sometimes we miss the mark and do something we should not. This is called life and being human. Do not be too hard on yourself, as long as you "learned" from the experience, consider it a "lesson learned."

There is not a magical formula to make you successful.

You will have to figure out the process that works for you. Learn from those who went before you.

There will be times of discouragement.

Discouragement can invade your own thoughts and come from the comments of others, so be prepared and do not let it influence you.

Are you ready to do what it takes?

If doing what it takes for success means waking up at 4am every day or staying up late every night are you prepared for that?

If doing what it takes requires you to watch less TV, less personal social media, or less time socializing (for a time), are you willing to do that?

If doing what it takes means you have to distance yourself from negative people are you ready to do that?

I never hang around negative people on a daily basis.

Realistically, it is impossible to remove all negative people from your life, but it does not mean you have to endure close relationships with them.

I wake up before the sun rises.

I plan my workday in advance with the intention of accomplishing goals.

During my business hours, I do my best to live my life on a schedule.

I know when I should wake up; go to work, and all the tasks I have to accomplish that day. After work hours, I try to be spontaneous and have personal time for family, friends, hobbies and relaxation. Doing this helps me keep a positive balance in my life.

I am willing to consult with and learn from someone who is smarter than I am.

I have learned to shut up and listen. If I meet someone who is smarter and more successful in a particular area than me, I choose to learn from him or her instead of being prideful or envious and competing with them.

I never have to be the most successful or smartest person in the room. I have nothing to prove to anyone.

In life, the only person I compete with is myself, challenging myself to do better in life.

I had to understand that no one is perfect in everything.

I have experienced failure and success. I learned from my failures and valued my successes.

I have learned to shut off my business mind and relax.

I have found that scheduling some relaxation time helps me come back to work more focused and energized.

I fully understand that some things will happen that I have no control over.

I simply cannot please every single person in my life, whether business or personal.

I have dreams and goals for the near and distance future.

I write them down and write out the steps I will take to achieve them.

I do not focus on long-term goals.

I focus on achieving short-term goals that lead to achieving long-term goals.

Your dreams and goals are achievable by taking the right steps towards them.

A good business idea is sometimes merely just an idea.

Every time an idea pops in my head is not a green light to start a new business. If that were the case, I would own about 1,000 different ice cream stands.

Almost never, agree immediately to a deal or terms unless it aligns with what you expected. If not, take time to back away and think things through.

Following my heart can sometimes get me in trouble.

How many times have you purchased something that you never used? At the time, it seemed perfect, nonetheless; it ended up just being a feeling that only lasted a few moments.

Never make important decisions when feeling overwhelmed with emotion.

It is not a failure as long as you learned something from it.

True success is not only measured by how much money you have but is defined by how much love, peace, and joy you give and receive.

Focus on problem solving, and seizing the opportunities that are right in front of you.

You will only go as far as you can believe, so believe BIG!

A good leader has followers; *a great leader produces other leaders.*

 *On a Personal Note,*

My desire is for everyone who is willing to put in the work to succeed in business.

Here are a few things to consider.

- You will be the one in-charge and the one who works the hardest for your business.

- No one will care about the success of your business more than you.

- You will be responsible for making the decisions that move your company forward.

- It is always best to invest in something that you possess passion and have vast knowledge about.

- Do not focus on making money. Instead, focus on providing an excellent product along with exceptional customer service and the money will come.

- You must be determined and ignore the critics. Let their doubts fuel you to push harder toward your goals.

- Before and after you start your business, you will have doubts: let your confidence always be greater than your doubts.

- If your business is experiencing loss only you can decide to stay strong and keep fighting or let go and move on to something else.

- Some people who you thought were your greatest supporters are likely to be the ones who fail to support you in the end.

- A number of people will envy and criticize your success.

- A few people who work for you, will be out for their own gain and not your company's success.

- In life, things that are worthy or valuable are rarely easy.

- Owning your business and being successful will not only give you financial independence, it will create a legacy for generations to come.

- It is possible for your dreams to become an actual reality.

- Be the best you can be.

- You are able to do whatever you put your mind and heart into.

- There is an opportunity all around us.

- Do not wait for the door to open instead, open it yourself.

- There will be ups and downs in life, choose not to stay down.

Study these words often as encouragement and a guide.

> *"I do not focus on long-term goals; I focus on achieving short-term goals that lead to achieving long-term goals."*

Chapter 5

Determining which Business is Right for You

"If you do something you love, you will always love doing it."

There are many people with a genuine desire to start a business and become financially independent; the problem is determining which type of business they should start. There are many different options to choose from. An example would be someone who loves food, preparation, cooking and seeing the smiles when someone loves their entrée, desert, or finger food would likely choose a business in the food industry.

A few options could be:

- Open a restaurant - a few choices are: Diner, Café, Deli, ToGo, Fast Food, Phone Order with delivery.

- Start a catering company.

- Use a food truck outside at social gatherings.

- Manufacture foods that sell to grocery stores, malls, airports, schools, government offices, etc.

How Some Well-Known Entrepreneurs Chose their Business

Example I

Several business owners choose a business type because they have worked in that industry for years and have a lot of knowledge and experience in the business.

Let's take Arthur Blank. He worked for a home improvement center for years and served as Vice President of finance. After years of service, he was fired. He took his experience and knowledge of the industry and co-founded the company we know today as Home Depot. (Luisa Kroll and Kerry A. Dolan)

Example II

Some business owners will try different business types until they find the business type that is a perfect fit for them.

Harland Sanders dabbled in the insurance and gas station business and eventually began selling fried chicken from his roadside restaurant. That fried chicken came to be the world's second largest restaurant chain (as measured by sales) known as KFC. (Sanders)

Example III

Some business owners will try a business opportunity in which they are passionate about.

Clarence Fender designed electric guitars, bass guitars, and amplifiers as a part of the global company we know today as Fender. In 1950, the "Fender Telecaster" was the first mass-produced solid body electric guitar. In 1992, Clarence Fender was inducted into the Rock and Roll Hall of Fame. The interesting thing about Clarence Fender was that he actually never learned how to play the guitar; he was just great at building them. (Frank Stroupe)

The common factor of all three entrepreneurs was they all loved what they did and were great at it.

"Choose a Business You are Passionate About"

Some of us are born with natural talents and abilities, while many have great passions: others learn and develop their skills and trades as the result of work experiences and/or through training from other people over the course of their lives. Choosing a business that you are passionate about will always be in your best interest, as passion will produce the patience, endurance, and strength needed in order to operate your business.

"Choose a Business You have Knowledge and Experience In"

IMPORTANT! Passion alone is not enough. Once you decide on the type of business you want to start, be sure that you have in-depth knowledge. Learn the history and milestone advancements that your industry has made. Learn what makes your industry necessary and the positive effect it has on society.

Study the large businesses in your industry and read how they started and how they got to where they are. I find it very interesting how many major corporations had humble beginnings. Most were just a hand full of people with ambition and a desire to follow their dreams.

With regards to experience I believe it is best to have some in the industry you choose. Especially if you have been successful as you will already have industry inside information, connections, and can avoid mistakes that you have previously learned in the past.

Some entrepreneurs have passion and knowledge, yet lack experience. For those, I would suggest you take slow and cautious steps and make careful decisions.

Every business owner will face challenges. However, they can be conquered if handled properly.

> *Sometimes mishaps are unavoidable but appropriate preparation is the key to minimizing them.*

"Choosing Your Business Type"

 **Interactive Exercises I-V**

Exercise I: Identifying your passion, knowledge and experience.

Let's take a moment to identify your natural talents and abilities or developed skills and trades.

Examples:

Culinary arts, the great outdoors, planning, working with children, swimming, construction, mechanical, fitness, education, technology, arts, fashion, design, sports, communication, gardening, oil and gas, chemistry and medicine.

Create your own list here:

_____

_____

_____

_____

_____

_____

_____

_____

_____

_____

Exercise II: List from greatest to least.

List in order from greatest to least, from the categories of your previous list in which you have the most knowledge, passion, and experience.

_____

_____

_____

_____

_____

_____

_____

_____

_____

_____

Exercise III: Turn your list into business types.

Consider your list and write down realistic business types that you could start. Start with the first three (3) items on your list.

Here are a few examples:

List:	Business Types:
Teaching	Tutoring Company, sell educational products.
Fitness	Cross Fit Gym, sell weight loss plans or products.
Communication	Human Resource, Consulting or Marketing firm.

_____

_____

_____

Exercise IV: Choosing your business type.

This exercise will help you determine which business type may be best for you. This can be narrowed down by answering these questions.

Which business type do you feel the most confident about?

_____

Which business type do you have the most passion, knowledge or experience in?

_____

What times and days are you able to work on your new business?

_____

Which business type works best when considering the time you have to spend on operating your business?

_____

How much money do you have to invest in your business? (More details on funding is covered in Chapter 14 titled, "Funding Your Business")

_____

Which business type will work when considering the funds you have available?

_____

The answer to these questions will give you an idea of which business type might be the best for you at this time. Your decision will ultimately depend on the passion, knowledge, experience, time and money you have to invest.

Choosing Lower Cost Options

If you want to start a business that requires start-up costs, which are considerably more than your available funding. Do not lose hope, because you are able to put your main business idea on hold and open a similar business type within your same industry with fewer start-up costs. Once the essential income has been made then you can use the funds on your main business idea. This option has worked before and is sometimes risky, as you never know how long it could take to make the required funds. On a positive note, you could end up with two businesses instead of one.

Example:

 Years ago, Joe, a friend of mine, came to me with his idea of starting a restaurant; he loved cooking. He was only free on weekends, and he did not have much money to invest or any assets that he could use to secure a small-business loan.

My advice to him was instead of opening a restaurant, to start a catering company. File the appropriate permits; sell his food to businesses, wedding and event planners, and the general public. When he saved up enough money, he could start the restaurant.

Although his heart was in opening a restaurant, it was not practical considering his circumstances, however, that did not mean it was impossible. He needed to take a few steps in a more realistic direction first, and when his circumstances changed, he could move forward toward his ultimate goal.

Exercise V: Time to make a final decision.

Put this book down and take a few hours to a few days to make your final decision on which business type you want to start. Think carefully of all your options, your answers to the questions, and remember that your choice does not have to be absolute: although, it will be double the work to go back and start all over. Though, it is better to do double work than lose out on investment income.

List your final business type here:

_____

Chapter 6

Understanding Your Business

"Make sure you know your business inside and out!"

Now that you have decided which business, you want to start, let's take some time and get to know your business.

All Businesses Offer a Product, a Service, or Both

A **product business** provides tangible goods that can be touched, sold, and transferred to the customer.

Examples: clothing, cell phone accessories, make-up, jewelry, automobiles, tools, building materials, computers, furniture, books, and etc.

A **service business** performs an act of service that you offer, sell, and complete for the customer.

Examples: hair stylist, designer, wedding planner, weight trainer, consulting, electronic repairs, realtors, etc.

Some businesses offer both products and services.

An example would be a hair salon that offers the service of cutting or styling hair plus the sale of hair products. Another example is an advertising agency that provides consulting advice (service) to businesses; and supplies printed media (products) to their customers for use as handouts.

Interactive Questions to Help You Understand Your Business

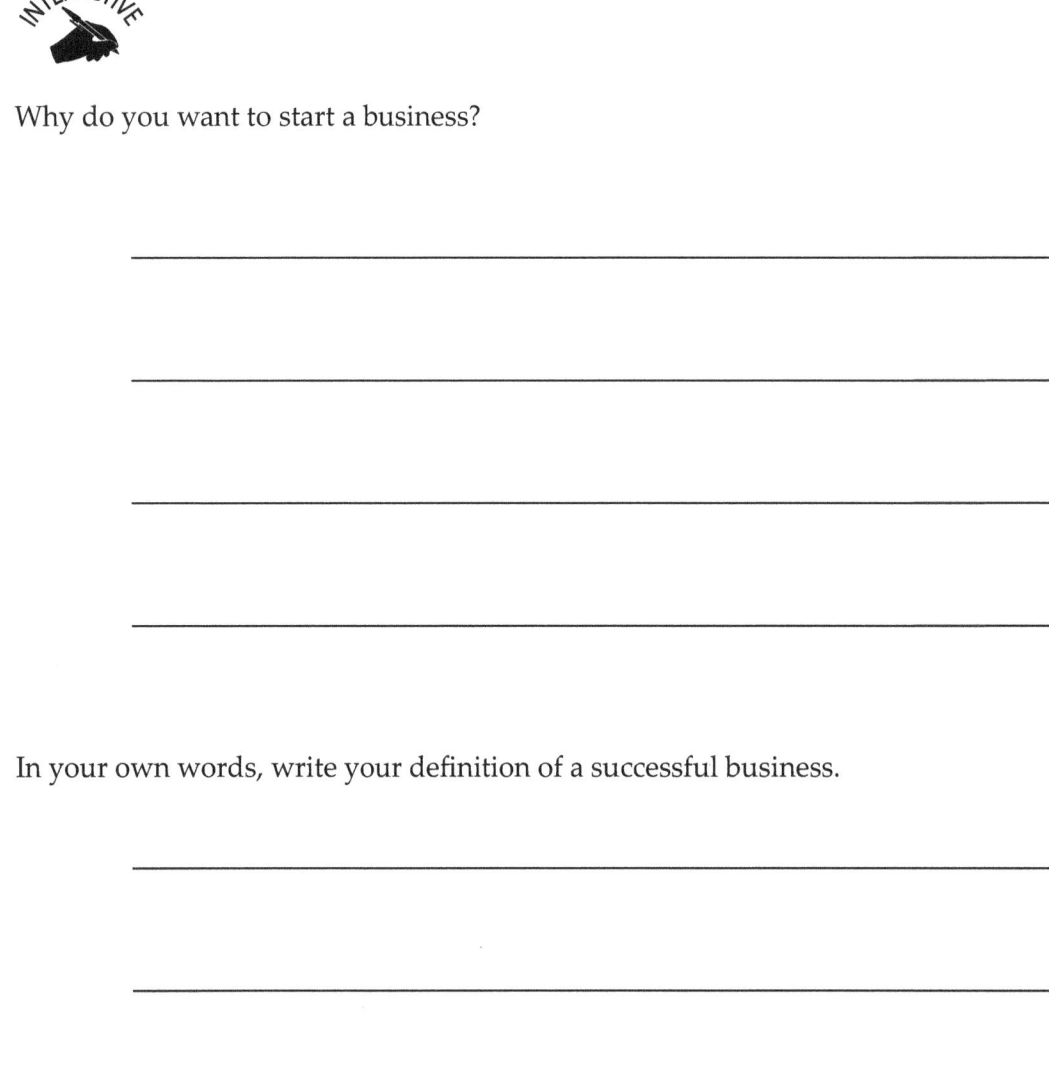

Why do you want to start a business?

_____

_____

_____

_____

In your own words, write your definition of a successful business.

_____

_____

_____

_____

Why did you choose your business idea?

_____

_____

_____

_____

On a scale from one to ten (10 being the highest) how passionate are you about your business idea?

_____

On a scale from one to ten (10 being the highest) how knowledgeable are you about your products and services?

_____

How many years' experience do you have in your business type?

_____

Products and Services

Will your business offer a product, service, or both?

_____

List the type of products or services you want to sell:

_____

_____

_____

What prices will you sell your products or services?

_____

_____

_____

_____

Why do people or other businesses need your products or services?

_____

_____

_____

_____

Is your product or service something that is required, necessary, or desired?

Circle one: Yes No

Required means your business offers a product or service that companies or individuals are required to purchase, either by law or by industry rules and regulations.

> An example would be vehicle insurance. All motor vehicles that operate within the US are required to obtain at minimum liability insurance.

Necessary means your business offers a product or service that companies or individuals need in order to operate.

> An example would be telecommunication services. Companies and individuals alike need a form of telecommunications to operate.

Desired means your business offers a product or service that companies or individuals choose to purchase, which result in a feeling or an emotion that brings satisfaction or enjoyment.

An example is operating a vacation/travel tour website or selling novelty items, both bring satisfaction or enjoyment to your customers.

Understanding which category your business falls under will help you when communicating with your customer base. You will be able to explain or give examples of the requirements, necessities, or enjoyment your products or services will provide.

Is your product or service something someone can purchase on impulse; or would they need time to think about the purchase, and possibly require financing?

_____

Examples:

Impulse – Clothing, Accessories, Office Supplies, Spa Treatments

Financing – Furniture, Landscaping Packages, Restaurant Supply, Vehicles

Is your business type a repeat business or one time purchase?

_____

Example:

Repeat – Clothing, Tech Support

One Time – Home-Moving Services

Competition

How Your Business Compares With Your Competition

List existing businesses that are the same type of business you want to start.

_____

_____

_____

_____

_____

What do you think makes them successful? Is it location, sales strategy, marketing campaigns, excellent customer service or all of the above?

_____

Why would a customer buy from you instead of them?

_____

_____

How do your prices compare to your competitors?

_____

_____

Are they the same, cheaper, more expensive and why?

_____

_____

_____

What will you offer or do differently than your competition?

_____

_____

_____

_____

Do not make the mistake of focusing too much on your competition but then again, not considering them is also a big mistake.

Believe it or not, there are similar business types out there with the sole intention of taking away your customer base and ultimately causing you to close your doors.

Make sure you know who your competition is; if you are successful enough, they will definitely know who you are.

When determining your prices, fees, and any other charges make sure they compete with other businesses that provide the same products or services as you.

Make sure you compare prices with companies who sell to your potential customers.

Example: If your business type is a high-end fashion boutique, you should compare your prices to other high-end fashion boutiques and not just another store that sells fashion clothing.

Location

Where will you operate your business? Home, office, warehouse, retail, kiosk, etc.

Side Note: For businesses that deal with the public.

Make sure your business is positioned in an area where the people who visit are most likely to buy your products or services.

Shipping & Delivery

After purchase, how long will it take a customer to receive your product or service?

_____

If they will not receive it immediately, what ways can you improve wait time?

_____

Know Your Seasons

What days of the week and/or seasons of the year, will your business make more sales?

_____

Example: Movie theaters and ice cream parlors have increased sales Friday, Saturday, and Sunday. Restaurants located in tourist locations have increased sales during summer months.

Knowing the Ins and Outs

Knowing the ins and outs of your business industry and type is extremely important before launching. You may be asked questions by customers concerning your industry and need to be ready to give answers on the spot. You need to know and commit to memory your products and services along with your prices and the prices your competition is charging.

You should know who the largest company in your industry is and how they got to where they are. You should research other companies who tried and failed in your industry and learn why.

Learn from other peoples mistakes.

Most of all love and enjoy what you do!

Who will Your Business Sell To?

<u>General Public Business</u> – Generally, any business that sells products or services to the general public. An example could be an insurance agency, restaurant, cell phone company or retail jewelry store.

<u>Business to Business</u> – Typically deals with other businesses and not to the general public. An example could be a jewelry vendor or manufacturer that makes or imports jewelry, then sells their products to jewelry stores who in turn sell to the public.

Other examples could be a phone equipment, hardware, brick, or restaurant supply company that supplies other businesses the products they need to sell or function.

<u>Specific Audience</u> – Refers to a business that provides products or services to a specific people group or industry. An example could be a business that provides diabetic and/or medical supplies to people who are in need of them or a business that sells oil field products to companies in the oil field industry.

This book is a perfect example of a specific business. You are reading this book because you want to either start a business or grow the business you currently operate. If you do not fall under those two categories this instructional handbook is of no use to you.

Know Your Customers

Knowing specifically to whom you are selling to is the first step in developing a marketing strategy to communicate with potential customers. Once you have identified your customers, learn how to communicate effectively with them. Understand what makes them decide to purchase and become repeat customers. More on this topic will be discussed in Chapter 21 titled, "Advertising & Marketing."

Establish Your Primary Products and Services

Establish a few primary products or services. Primary products or services are the leading top selling items that will bring you the most customers, sales, and profits.

Next, decide on your secondary-level products or services. Secondary-level products or services are offered as "add-ons" or useful items that complement the sale of primary products and/or services.

For example:

Primary Product – Electronics

Secondary Service – Warranty and Tech Support

Primary Service – Accounting Services

Secondary Service – Notary and Printing Services

Primary Product and Service – Flowers, Floral Arrangement, and Delivery
                                  Event Planning, and Catering

Secondary Product and Service – Greeting Cards, Balloons, and Set-up and Tear-Down Crews

If you had to choose a few primary products or services, what would they be and why?

(This question does not apply if you are only selling one item or one service.)

_____

_____

_____

The answer is helpful when placing advertisements. Too many products or services on an ad will make it appear cluttered and lack customer appeal.

List your secondary products or services.

_____

_____

_____

Company Culture

Company culture is the personality of a company and defines what a company, from an employee perspective, is like to work for. Company culture includes the company mission, values, ethics, expectations, goals, and work environment. (Doyle) Some companies have a team-based culture with employee participation on all levels, while others have a more traditional and formal management style.

Company Mission – Also known as a mission statement is a written declaration of an organization's core purpose and focus that normally remains unchanged overtime. (Business Dictionary)

It should answer these 3 questions:

What it does, who it does it for, and how?

Example: Our mission is to connect with customers on a personal level while offering them our products and services. We will treat every customer as an individual and not just a number by understanding and meeting their needs, as well as exceeding their expectations.

The mission statement for the business development division of Small Business Assistance of America is listed below.

"Our mission is to assist our customers with their new business start-up while keeping their costs as low as possible."

Values – Also known as Core Values is a person's principles or standards of behavior; one's judgment of what is important in life. (Google) It is exhibited with words or phrases that are meaningful and describe the characteristics and behavior of the company, its owners, and staff. (YourDicionary)

Every business should have a set of "Core Values" established as company operating guidelines.

Examples are:

Honesty	•	Loyalty	•	Innovative	•	Creative
Positive	•	Passionate	•	Dedication	•	Experience
Punctuality	•	Ambition				

Make sure you and your staff conduct business keeping your core values in mind.

Ethics – Moral principles that govern a person's or group's behavior. (Google)

Explained - Your Company ethics may be fairness, honesty, innovation, loyalty, patience, honor, etc.

70

Expectations – a belief that someone will or should achieve something. (Google)

> Explained - Let your employees know what you expect from them and ensure you set the "ideal" example. Have a written list of the job duties your employees are expected to perform on a daily or project basis and give deadlines. Let them know their behavior at work should reflect the company's culture.

Goals for Employees – the object of a person's ambition or effort; an aim or desired result. (Google)

> Explained - Let your employees know your short and long term goals. Set monthly sales goals and reward when they are achieved.

Work Environment – Location where a task is completed. (Business Dictionary)

> Explained - It also involves other factors such as the atmosphere of the work environment, which could be friendly, relaxed, slow or fast paced, hostile, deadline driven, etc.

 Listed below are a few tips to create a healthy company culture:

1. Stay positive - even in the face of opposition, mistakes, and workplace disagreements.

2. Treat your employees and customers with respect.

3. Make sure voice tones of employees are friendly and not demanding.

4. Be the example of the type of employee you wish to hire.

5. Hire people who line up with the values of your company.

6. Hire people who agree and support your company's vision.

7. Teach your staff to never assume – always ask and get clarity.

8. Make sure to praise and encourage your employees on a frequent basis.

9. Learn to trust your employees with tasks without constantly checking on them.

10. Train employees so well that they are able to train others.

11. Stress the importance of customer service.

12. Ask for and be open to feedback from employees and customers.

13. Constantly share your company's culture with your employees to make sure everyone is in alignment with your company.

Take some time and write the company culture you desire for your business. It does not need to be complete and you are able to revisit this section and complete it at a later time. However, I do advise you have it completed before opening day or before hiring employees.

Once you hire employees, make sure to share it with them on a consistent basis. Keep in mind that your company culture will not be confined to the workplace among employees but will be on display for your customers to see when you or your team interacts with them.

INTERACTIVE   Company Culture:

_____

_____

_____

_____

_____

Vision

The Vision for your company is an overview of what your business intends to offer as a whole, to your customers now and in the future.

Here is a generic example of a vision statement.

Our vision is to provide an excellent product and service to our customers at an affordable price while providing a great customer service experience.

Here is the vision statement for Small Business Assistance of America.

"Our vision is to teach and equip business owners by providing step by step instruction to develop a realistic plan and business strategy."

Write your vision statement here.

_____

_____

_____

_____

_____

_____

Business Goals

It is very important as a business owner that you *list a few attainable goals within a specific period*. Once you reach your goals, begin a new list of goals by challenging yourself with slightly greater numbers.

For example:

If you sell insurance, you might want to set a goal list somewhat like this.

First month - make at least 15 solid connections with potential clients.

Second month - make at least 6 insurance contracts while making 17 solid connections with additional potential clients.

Third month - make at least 9 insurance contracts while making 20 solid connections with additional potential clients.

Another example:

If you were a weight loss consultant or a hair stylist, your goal list would look like this.

First month – pass out 1,000 business cards to potential clients, offer ½ off for new customers.

Second month - book at least 10 clients, pass out 1,000 business cards to potential clients, offer 40% off for new customers.

Third month - book at least 15 clients, pass out 1,000 business cards, offer 30% off to new clients.

 Make a list of goals and use it as a guide to stay on track and keep focused. If you meet your goals too quickly, increase your goal limits. If you do not meet your goals, keep going until you do, or you may need to change the way you are representing your product or service.

Write down your goals list here.

_____

_____

_____

_____

_____

_____

_____

Do not let Big Business Intimidate You

There may be several large corporations in the same industry and business type as you. They may have a great number of employees and office, retail, or warehouse space. The truth is that conceivably years ago when they started out, they were a small business just like you. They found the processes that worked for them, had a plan, and were not afraid of change and growth followed.

Look around at existing large businesses and see how small business can still operate despite their size. Some customers would rather go to local small businesses to avoid long lines and wait times. Others go because they wish to receive a more personalized service, which they feel cannot be given by larger companies.

We can point out credit unions, boutiques, small grocery stores, etc. They all exist and still function although there are large corporations offering the same products or services. So do not let large business intimidate you, instead learn from them and let them inspire you.

Checklist before Moving Forward in this Book

At this point, you should know the following:

- ✓ Which type of business you want to start.

- ✓ Why you want to start a business.

- ✓ Steps to developing a positive mindset.

- ✓ Ingredients that lead to a successful business.

- ✓ Company Culture.

- ✓ Products and/or services you are offering.

- ✓ Pricing.

- ✓ Know who your competitors are.

- ✓ Competition's pricing.

- ✓ Primary products or services.

- ✓ Secondary products or services.

- ✓ Specific details about your business.

- ✓ Know your customers.

- ✓ Vision and Mission.

- ✓ Short Term Goals.

(Do not proceed until you are able to check all of the items listed)

Chapter 7

Be Aware of Critics and Negative People

"A successful person can be certain of this;
there will never be a shortage of critics"

I chose to position this chapter early because I want to inform you of what can happen in the business world.

Be careful with whom you share your dreams, goals, and vision. Not everyone will be as excited and supportive as you want him or her to be. When I first started in business, there were plenty of negative comments and criticisms, so I learned quickly not to listen or let it consume me.

You have a choice to make when negative people approach you and they are likely to do so. You cannot let their negative words sway your decision to start your business, you must move forward in confidence. Generally, I only speak of my personal business matters with other business owners who are successful and in non-competing businesses.

An Inescapable Reality

Any business owner, who has been in business for a few years and experienced success, has felt the sting of criticism and verbal negativity. I wish there was a way that everyone would just get along; however, that is not how it works in the real business world. You may be subjected to criticism among people or other businesses either through your successes or through your failures.

If your business is experiencing success, others may try to copy your business idea or steal your strategy and become your competition. It has happened to many business owners and

I hope it never happens to you. If you are experiencing loss or a slow season, others may be glad to see your business suffering. Sadly, some people let envy, anger, pride, etc. get the best of them, and it will cause them to act in ways they normally would not.

Any successful business person who is at the top of their industry will tell you that you do not reach the top, without some people trying to pull you down.

Remember, you cannot let the actions or opinions of others dictate who you are and what you will do in life. You were put on this earth for a reason and if entrepreneurship is in your heart, then go for it! Decide for yourself what you will believe. I choose to believe positively and will push forward toward my goals despite the doubts and criticisms of others.

Final Advice

Everyone has an opinion, be mindful of the negative ones.

Never take advice from a negative person because all you will get is negative advice.

> *Doubts and distractions
> are the enemies of success.*

Chapter 8

Choosing a Business Name & Entity Type

"You want a name people will remember."

Your business name and its overall look (shape and color) will make an immediate impression on whoever comes across it.

It will be displayed on your retail storefront, office door, website, business cards, brochures, and other marketing materials, etc. When customers call, your employees will answer the phone using your business name. After a customer has purchased your products your business name will be on receipts and packaging.

When customers talk about your business to others, your business name will be the start of their conversation. With this in mind, make sure the immediate impression your business name gives is a positive one.

When it comes to choosing a business name there are several choices and for some it could take days to even weeks to make a final decision. This chapter has categorized business names, giving you examples, and questions to answer along with tips to help you decide on a perfect name for your new business.

Business Name Categories

Business name choices generally fall into one of these categories:

1. Use your first or last name in the business title, initials or both. Example: James Cash Penny founded JC Penney in 1902. (Penny)

2. Use one, two or three words as the business name or join them to make one name. Example: Staples, Simply Fashion, Creation Works, Facebook, Microsoft.

3. Utilizing acronyms is another category. Join several words together and taking the first letter of each word to form a name. Example: IHOP refers to International House of Pancakes while UFC refers to Ultimate Fighting Championship.

4. Combine a first or last name with a common word in your specific industry. Example: Using Smith Logistics creates a solid name for a shipping company. Joe's Pizza lets people know what type of food service is available.

5. Another option is to use an entirely made-up name using letters that are not normally together.

Example: Google or Yahoo

Business Names You Remember

INTERACTIVE Make a list of existing business names that easily come to mind.

Example: Target, IHOP, JC Penney, etc.

_____

_____

_____

_____

_____

_____

_____

What is it about these names that make you remember them?

Is it their color, shape, word placement, or something else?

_____

_____

_____

Which business names are clear as far as what they offer?

_____

_____

_____

Which business names have their industry added to their business name?

Example: Smith Logistics, Sam's Burgers & Fries.

_____

_____

_____

Write down the choice category listed at the beginning of this chapter for each business name.
Example: IHOP - acronym.

_____

_____

_____

_____

_____

The answers to the questions give you an idea of businesses that you have interacted with or come across that have stood out to you in such a way that you can remember them instantly. They were able to make a lasting impression on you, which should be your goal when choosing your business name. Learn from their examples and choose your business name wisely.

Tips on Choosing a Business Name

Here are a few tips, to keep in mind when choosing your business name.

Using one, two or three words separate or together for a business name is great for branding. Keep it simple, easy to understand, and easy to remember. What may be more challenging is making sure the domain name (website business name) is available and is not currently registered. Also, if your industry is not specified you will need to follow the rule of a creative slogan, logo, and/or have an effective advertising/marketing campaign.

Making use of acronyms can be interesting and unique when joining letters together and forming a new or existing word. Make sure the word formed is something people can easily remember and spell. You will also want to have the meaning of your acronym fully displayed for customers to read. You can list company core values or industry specific words within your acronym or you can list characteristics that are meaningful to you. Your options are limitless as long as the final acronym is easy to recall accurately.

A common word within your specific industry is a great way for people to find your business. This is especially beneficial when utilizing online search engines to search for products or services. If you own an auto supply store named Reese Auto Supply, when potential customers search for "auto supplies", your company may pull up under local listings by default because of the word "supply" in your business name. (This assumes you registered your business online. You will receive more details in another chapter concerning online registration options.) It also provides customer advantage by having an idea of what products or services you offer just by reading your business name. Example business name: Mark's Deli,

Slogan: Serving Sandwiches, Soups, & Smiles since 1953

Using a completely made up name is a unique option as long as the name is easy to read, spell, and pronounce. You will have the added benefit of no one mistaking your business name with another business. Chances are there will be no problems when registering your business name on the Internet (domain name) and no problems if you choose to Trademark your business name (which is highly suggested if you choose this category).

You will have to work hard when letting the public or other businesses know what type of industry you are in. A solution would be using your industry, products, or services in your logo, slogan, or having an effective advertising/marketing program. Choosing this category can be a lot of fun or very nerve-racking, so take your time and carefully consider your choices and options.

The physical location of your business may be in a retail setting, mall or store kiosk, office building, warehouse, stand-alone structure, or even your own home. Regardless of your location, your business name will most likely be what your customers see first and positive first impressions are the key to creating interest and obtaining potential customers.

 Before you choose a business name, look around and notice the different businesses. Note the ones that inspire you or you can easily remember. Learn from their example and see which category they chose when deciding their business name.

Choose Your Business Name

Take a moment to think of a few names for your business. You can list a few names from each category listed at the beginning of this chapter. It is always a good idea to come up with a few different names just in case your desired business name is already taken.

Key points to think about:

- Is it easy to spell?

- Is it easy to remember?

- How easy can someone find you on a search engine?

- Does your business name reflect what your company offers or would you rather put that information in your logo or slogan?

 List three different business names here. This could take anywhere from a few hours to a few days. It is all right to take your time on this.

_____

_____

_____

Two major factors to remember when choosing your business name:

- Is my business name available for registration in my county or state?

- Is my business name available for registration on the Internet?

Note: *If you are using SmallBusinessAA.com to help register your business there will be assistance with determining registration availability.*

Once availability has been determined, you will need to choose one business name.

> "When customers talk about your business to others, your business name will be the start of their conversation."

List one business name here:

_____

Choosing an Entity Type

Now that you have chosen your business name, let's go over the three most common entity types for new business owners.

- Assumed Name (DBA-Doing Business As),

- Limited Liability Company (LLC),

- S Corporation (Inc.)

There are also Professional Service Corporations and Professional Limited Liability Companies, which traditionally pertain to individuals with a special license to operate within a specific industry. An example would be doctors or lawyers.

Assumed Name or DBA (Doing Business As) is one of the most common and simple forms to start a business immediately. (Wikipedia) This is accomplished by registering your business name (after checking availability) at your local County Clerk's office. The cost can be low depending on the county where you are registering your name. You can do it in person or by mail. Let's say your name is Michelle Smith, once you register an assumed name you are stating that Michelle Smith is now "Doing Business As" _____ (your business name).

Things you should consider when choosing an Assumed Name as your entity type

This is the simplest and lowest cost of forming a business.

Your business can begin immediately, you are qualified to have customers, and banks recognize you as a legitimate business.

You are personally responsible for all debts and obligations of the company. If your business is sued for any reason, you will be personally responsible for paying the debt. If you were to purchase general liability insurance, your insurance company may pay the debt for you, up to the insured amount; providing the lawsuit falls under your coverage. General liability insurance is discussed further in Chapter 30 titled, "Taxes, Expenses, and Business Insurance."

Example: Let's say you own a candy store called Mike's Candy Store (DBA). You own a home, cars, a house full of furniture and $7,000 in your personal savings account. Your business is in a retail location with $5,000 worth of equipment and inventory.

A child walks into your store with his mother and both of them slip and fall because your employee did not clean up a water spill. They are both rushed to the hospital to find out the mother suffered a broken arm and leg after the fall. She chooses to sue you to cover the cost of medical bills which totaled $30,000.

If you had a sufficient insurance policy and the accident was covered in the terms of your policy, then it should cover the medical bills. However, if you did not have an insurance policy then you would be liable to pay the medical bills in full. If you did not have the money to pay for them the judge, may require your business equipment be sold, deplete your personal savings account, sell your vehicles, etc. until they are paid.

Extremely
IMPORTANT → I cannot express enough the necessity for business insurance policies.

If you have a business partner both of you will have to be present in order to file an Assumed Name with your County Clerk's office or local governing authority. The standard registration period of an Assumed Name is usually ten years. After ten years, you will have to register it again. You will not be taxed as a separate entity but will add the "profits or losses" to your personal federal tax return based on your ownership percentages.

A **Limited Liability Company** gives you added liability protection against any debts or lawsuits (Random House). Which means if you are sued you will not be personally liable for the debts but your business will be. If you have general liability insurance, your insurance company will determine if the lawsuit debt is covered under your policy.

This option costs more than an Assumed Name but adds personal liability protection.

You have a minimum two-week waiting period after you submit your paperwork (varies from state to state) to receive an official "filed with the state" approval by mail to start your business.

You may be seen as a more established business as it will be registered with your state. Once you register an LLC it will remain active until you choose to terminate it.

You will not be taxed as a separate entity, but instead you will add the "profits or losses" to your personal federal tax return based on your ownership percentages.

An **S Corporation** is an independent legal entity owned by shareholders. The corporation itself is held liable for its actions and debts. It is a complex business structure because of its legal filing requirements. You must first file for a "traditional corporation" then file for S Corporation status. (William Perez)

This option sometimes cost more to register than an LLC (depending on state); however, it adds liability protection and tax savings. You can have one or multiple shareholders (owners) and can sell ownership in the corporation through stock offerings. This is the preferred entity type for investors and "going public" (placing your business on the stock market).

If S Corp status is granted the business's profits and losses are added to your personal federal income tax. You have a tax savings advantage over Assumed Names and LLCs since they are liable for employment taxes on their entire net income. While, S Corporations pay employment taxes only on wages (paychecks) and not the entire net income (earnings after expenses). Self-Employment taxes are Medicare and Social Security payments that are deducted from your paycheck.

Example:

Assumed Name/LLC	$100K	$50K	Paid on total $100K	$15,300
Business Type	**Net Income**	**Paycheck**	**Self-Employment Tax 15.3%**	**Cost**
S Corp	$100K	$50K	Paid only on $50K	$ 7,600

Differences

This chart outlines some differences between Assumed Names, Limited Liability Companies, and S Corps.

Benefit	Assumed Name	LLC	S Corp
Liability Protection	No	Yes	Yes
Owner Cash Withdrawals	Yes	Yes	No
Self-Employment Tax on Net	Yes	Yes	No
Investor Preferred	No	No	Yes
Payroll Processing	Only if you have employees	Only if you have employees	Yes

With an Assumed Name or an LLC you are able to withdraw what you pay yourself from your business bank account. These withdrawals are called "owner withdrawals" and will be considered as net income at the end of the year. With an S Corp you will need to set up formal payroll processing and file employment taxes quarterly.

 Regardless of the entity you choose make sure you have at minimum, a general liability insurance policy in place.

Carefully consider your options then list your Entity Type here.

Registering Your Business

If you wish to register an Assumed Name, you may do so by contacting your local County Clerk's office. There is no need to pay additional fees and have someone register it for you. You will only need to show an I.D. and have your business name available when registering.

Follow these steps to register an Assumed Name.

1. Visit your local County Clerk's office or governing authority.

2. Bring your ID and all business owners must be present.

3. Make sure your desired business name is available.

As far as LLC, S Corporation and other entity types are concerned, I strongly suggest you do not file on your own. Preferably, have a person or company that has experience in that field do it for you. The extra cost will be worth it when it comes to making sure it is filed correctly if any legal issues ever arise.

Operating Agreements & Bylaws

State law requires all corporations to have a document stating their organization and day-to-day operations. The document is called corporate bylaws.

Corporate bylaws generally consist of:

*   The structure of the organization

*   The duties and responsibilities of a corporation's members

*   Details about the board of directors

*   Information about when and where directors' and shareholders' meetings will be held

Limited liability companies (LLCs) in many states are required to create an LLC operating agreement.

LLC operating agreements consist of:

- Members' percentages of ownership

- Members' rights and responsibilities

- Members' voting powers

- Allocation of profits and losses

- Management details

Corporations and LLCs are not required to file their bylaws or operating agreements with the Secretary of State.

One of our goals at Small Business Assistance of America is to help you get your business registered promptly and efficiently, while keeping cost as low as possible.

Visit SmallBusinessAA.com for more information concerning Business Registration, Website Development & Online Store, Domain Name (website name), Business Email, Credit Card Processing, Graphic Design & Advertising Materials.

(Read Chapter 9: <u>Domain Name & Web Hosting</u>

before registering your business)

Chapter 9

Website and Online Store Setup

"24 hours, 7 days a week – your website is always OPEN For Business"

In times past when consumers searched for a business, they turned to telephone books, now consumers turn to the Internet. Making sure your business is registered on Internet search engines and having a website for consumers to view will increase your chances of being noticed and make more sales.

Websites play such an important role when communicating your products and services to your potential customers. You are able to provide exact detailed descriptions of what you offer along with any additional information your customers may need 24 hours a day, 7 days a week.

Having your business registered on popular search engines like Google.com, Yahoo.com, Bing.com, Yelp.com, Yellowpages.com, etc. will allow customers to find your business when searching for the products and services you offer.

Here is how it works;

Domain Name & Website

Once you have decided on a business name you will then need to determine if that name or an abbreviation of it is available to register as a domain name. In reference to business, a "Domain Name" is a registered business name on the Internet that leads to your website.

Example: www.MyNewBizName.com (We can help you determine availability if necessary.)

 ***Note:*** *Before you register your business with your county or state, it is extremely important that you check to see if your domain business name is available and try to register them both about the same time.*

When your business is in operation, you will want to have a website up and running. This gives prospective customers access to learn more about your products, services, location, hours of operation, and to make purchases. For examples of how you want your website to look go online, look at several existing websites, and see the different design layouts and options.

 ***Note:*** *The more extensive a website looks, usually means the more it costs.*

The main colors of your website should be consistent with the colors you choose for your business name, logo, and advertisement graphics. Doing so will give customers the same look and feel when interacting with you.

Choosing Your Website Menu Tabs

Websites usually have navigational tabs (menus) on the top and/or left side of the site. This gives customers options as to what they want to view or learn more about while maneuvering within a site.

Some common tab names are:

- Home

- About Us

- Products

- Services

- Pricing

- Contact Us

Website Photos & Graphics

Your website should have photos and graphics consistent with your business type. There are a variety of stock photos your website designer can use. If you choose to use your own photos be sure they are taken with a high quality camera.

 Make sure to have photos of your products, along with a description that includes size and weight. In this way, customers have an idea of what to expect when purchasing your products.

If you are a service business then you can have photos or graphics that show what your services consist of.

Testimonials and Experience

If you have a few customer testimonies make sure to add them to your website. Testimonies can consist of customers' interaction with your overall business or their satisfaction with your products or services.

If you have extensive experience in your business type, add that information on your website as well. Detail how many years of experience, what accomplishments you have made, and any other information that will give your customers a sense of security when interacting with your business.

Credentials

If you are licensed, have degrees or awards pertaining to your business then make sure to add that information on your website.

Social Media

Your business should be registered with the social media accounts that your customers are most likely using. Examples are Facebook, Instagram, Twitter, Pinterest, etc. Add links on your website that direct customers to your social media pages.

Have a Responsive Website

I suggest a website that is known as responsive. This means it is easily viewable on multiple screen sizes of computers as well as mobile devices. Many customers use cell phones and tablets to look up businesses instead of laptops or desktop computers in today's advancing technical world.

Not Website Savvy? It's OK, we are here to help!

If you are not website savvy it is OK, we offer domain name registration and website development services.

We will do most of the work for you!

 Visit SmallBusinessAA.com for more information concerning Business Registration, Website Development & Online Store, Domain Name (website name), Business Email, Credit Card Processing, Graphic Design & Advertising Materials.

There are several other domain registration and website development companies to choose from. If you have experience in this field, you already know your options. If not, please choose wisely when determining which service to use.

Some companies provide websites for free or for a few dollars a month, however, you have to build the site yourself. If you are not experienced, you may find yourself spending countless hours trying to figure out how to develop your website instead of focusing on operating your business. Remember, you get what you pay for.

Tips on Domain Registration

 Tip 1: Register your business name and domain at or about the same time
It is suggested (not required) you search availability and register your business name on the Internet (the domain name) at or about the same time, you register your business name. Not doing this could result in your domain name not being available. Moreover, you may have to decide on another domain name or business name.

An example would be registering Smith Logistics without checking to see if that name was an available domain name. You will soon find out that www.SmithLogistics.com, (.net, .org, .biz) is taken; therefore, you might have to register a different business name or register www.MySmithLogistics.com, www.SmithLogisticsUSA.com or something similar.

 Tip 2: Register Multiple Domain Extensions

Furthermore, it is suggested that you should register other popular extensions for your website, not only the dot com (.com).

Other popular extensions are:

.net	.info	.co	.us
.org	.tv	.biz	.guru

If you do not register multiple domains someone else can buy your other domain extensions and develop a website with advertisements from other companies in the same industry. Which may confuse your potential customers as to which one is your real site. The advertisements may even be your actual local competitors. They can make money every time someone clicks on an advertisement and directs your potential customers to other similar sites and away from yours.

Many business owners learn this the hard way so I am advising you beforehand of this possibility.

Example: Business name – MyNewBiz, LLC

Popular Domain Extensions are - .com .net .co .org .info .biz .us

Let's say you only buy the .com then someone else can buy the .net and .org and develop a website with industry information concerning the business type along with ads that lead to other websites.

My suggestion is to buy all popular available domain extensions or at least the .com, .net and the .org, however, the choice is yours.

 *Note: If you choose to run your business without a website, please understand that you will lose out on prospective business. It also suggests to potential customers that you lack the appearance of a professional organization.*

 Small Business Assistance of America Web Registeration Services

Your main goal is to get your business up and running. In all probability, you do not have time to learn everything there is to know about registering domain names and developing websites. We want you to focus on other preparation tasks for your business. We initiated a website development service to help get your website up and running.

Our service options include:

- Registering your business domain name.

- Website design.

- Logo design.

- Business email.

- Setting up your online store, if applicable.

- Assist in setting-up your business to accept credit cards.

- Graphic design and advertising materials.

- And more!

> *"Our desire is to get your business up and running on the Internet as soon as possible and in a cost-effective manner. This allows you to focus on your business and start making sales."*

Chapter 10

Sales Tax, EIN, Licensing & Permits

"The 'must haves' in order to operate"

Every business has different rules and regulations they must abide by. Listing every one of them could take a lifetime, so I have decided to give you general information concerning the most common "must haves" businesses need in order to operate.

Regardless of your entity type, your business may be required by your county, state, or federal government to have certain regulated and/or posted permits or notices while in operation.

Listed below is a breakdown of what your business may need in order to operate.

Sales Tax Permit

Sales tax is a tax imposed by the government at the point of sale on retail goods and services. (Investopedia)

Sales tax permits are required for businesses who sell taxable products or services in order to collect sales tax from your customers. To determine if you are required to collect sales tax for your products or services you must view your state's website page concerning sales tax or simply call their sales tax department. Please be aware that if your business is required to have a sales tax permit and you chose to operate without one, it will result in fines and penalties.

Once you have determined if your products or services are taxable, you must apply for a sales tax permit and start collecting sales tax.

Sales tax information and applying for permits can be found by doing an online search for "sales tax permit for _____ (list your state)". Click on the link that is from your states official website.

Before applying, you will need to know your industry code, also known as NAICS. The North American Industry Classification System (NAICS) is the standard used by Federal statistical agencies in classifying business establishments for the purpose of collecting, analyzing, and publishing statistical data related to the U.S. business economy. (Census.gov)

 In short, it is a code used by the government to categorize your business. Your sales tax permit application will require it. You can locate your company's code by visiting http://www.census.gov/eos/www/naics/.

Collecting Sales Tax

I suggest using a software program or cash register that will help calculate the percentage amount to be collected and has the ability to run reports detailing how much sales tax was collected.

Example on collecting sales tax if your rate is 8.25%:

Product or Service cost $125

Sales Tax ($125 X 8.25%) = 10.31

Total to be charged to customer ($125 + 10.31) = $135.31

$125 belongs to your business while $10.31 belongs to your sales tax governing agency.

It is extremely important to keep your sales figures separate from the amounts collected for sales tax.

Some businesses obtain a separate bank account exclusively for the sales tax collected. By making deposits weekly, they can be assured they do not consider the amounts as business income and have the sufficient funds when they remit their taxes. Other businesses will keep the sales tax and business income in the same account yet have it separated in accounting reports.

IMPORTANT! Whichever you decide make sure that you do not spend the sales tax collected. When it is time to report and pay your governing agency the sales tax you collected, they will expect payment in full. If you are unable to send payment in full, it could result in fines, penalties, liens, and possible collection of your business property.

Reporting and Paying Collected Sales Tax

Sales tax payments are generally made quarterly to your governing agency. Once you register for a sales tax permit you should start receiving quarterly notices or forms in the mail asking how much your sales were and how much of your sales were considered taxable. You need to report these amounts for all your business locations. Then perform a few calculations, which will determine how much sales tax you owe (collected tax from your customers). You will be guided as to which calculations you need to perform on the form or notice you receive.

Your governing agency will have a phone number you can call for assistance on filling out the form. Once you have made the appropriate calculations you will be ready to list a final total sales tax due and send payment before the due date.

Sales tax permits must be posted for customers to view unless otherwise instructed by your governing agency.

Since sales tax permits are considered "public information" other businesses will be able to access your information and will call the phone number you list on your application to solicit their services.

Other Common Permits

Occupancy Permit

Occupancy permits also known as a "Certificate of Occupancy" is a certificate issued from a local governing agency indicating that a building adheres to the local building codes and is ready for occupancy, generally a prerequisite to taking possession. (yourdictionary.com)

If you decide to lease commercial space for your business, you may be required to file for an occupancy permit (Certificate of Occupancy). Filing this permit initiates a visit from your local governing agency. They will determine if the space you desire to lease meets the local building codes for electrical, fire safety, exit signs, etc. The assessment also identifies how many people your business space can safely house at one time.

Upon passing inspection, you will be issued a permit or certificate which will be posted for customers to view unless otherwise instructed by the governing agency.

Your building manager should be able to notify you if you are required to file for this permit or certificate. If not, you must contact your local governing agency by doing an online search for "certificate of occupancy in _____ (list your city and state).

Sign Permit

A sign permit is written approval by your local governing agency stating your sign meets their criteria for allowing signage on commercial property.

Generally, if you are leasing a retail location and adding a sign to the property, you will need a sign permit. Sign permits are usually issued to the licensed sign contractor who will be constructing and installing your sign. After installation, the sign contractors will then handover the permit to you. Your commercial property management will notify you verbally or give you their written guidelines for your sign. The licensed sign contractor you hire should be able to provide you the City's rules and guidelines for signage.

To find a licensed sign contractor do an Internet search for "signs in _____(list your city)".

EIN

Employer Identification Number

EIN- A unique identification number that is assigned to a business entity so that they can easily be identified by the Internal Revenue Service. (Investopedia) An EIN (Employer Identification Number) can be looked at as a social security number for your business and is commonly used for the following reasons:

- If you have employees – Your payroll company will use this number to submit to payroll taxes to the IRS.

- Used to open a bank account – When you open a personal bank account they require your social security number. The same goes when you open up a business bank account, they will use your EIN number.

- Federal Tax ID – If a business pays you for products or services they may ask for a Federal Tax ID number so when they file their taxes they can report those payments to the IRS. A Federal Tax ID is the same number as an EIN.

- Your EIN is also used when filing federal income taxes.

An EIN number is required for an S Corporation and optional for an Assumed Name or Limited Liability Company. I highly suggest you file for an EIN so you do not have to give out your social security number as an alternative. EINs usually do not require posting for public view.

In order to apply for an EIN you simply have to do an online search for "applying for an EIN" and select the link that begins with www.IRS.gov.

Licensing

Licensing – a license is proof that an individual was instructed in a specific field, tested and passed state requirements which granted approval to operate in a specific industry or field. Whether or not a license is required to operate your business will depend on your specific industry field. Anywhere from a hair stylist to a plumber including most contractor industries will need a license. If you went to school to learn your trade, your instructor should have the information you need to apply for your license.

If you know a trade due to your experience and not the result of a formal education, you may need to check with your city or county government office to verify your eligibility to operate in that field without having spent time in a classroom or having a license.

Final Advice

It is extremely important that you make sure your business is compliant with all county, state, or federal requirements before and during the operation of your business. Not doing so could result in fines, penalties and the possible closure of your company.

Chapter 11

Choosing a Logo & Slogan

"You want to grab your customers' attention and have them remember you by impulse."

Logos have been used for years as a unique image to get customers to remember and recognize your business. Slogans have been used to deliver a quick yet important message to your customers. They both have proven to be very effective when marketing your business.

Let's get started.

Question: Is it 100% necessary to have a logo or slogan?

No, not at all, in fact, several successful businesses exist with only a business name.

Some companies simply use their business name uniquely written as their logo.

Having a logo and/or a slogan can provide your customers with something to recognize your company. As a new business, I would definitely suggest using a logo, a slogan, or both.

Logos

A company logo speaks to your customers without any words. It should rarely ever be changed since customers will develop recognition by seeing it on your advertisements, memos, emails, products, packaging, among other items. This process is known as branding. Nearly all companies will retain the same logo for multiple years before changing or updating it.

Let's complete a short exercise:

Do not do any research or ask anyone for help. Take a moment to think about the products or companies that you recognize just by their logo.

An example would be McDonald's, their logo (golden arches) stands out from far away.

> "You want to grab your customers' attention and have them remember you by impulse."

In addition, list businesses that use their business name as their logo.

An example would be Google, Facebook, and many major department stores, like JC Penney or Macy's.

INTERACTIVE List them here: Companies you can recognize just by their logo and companies that use just their business name as their logo.

_____

_____

_____

_____

_____

_____

What about their logos or business name made you recognize them? Was it the colors, the shape; was it simple, creative, how frequently you have seen it, or something else?

"A Company logo speaks to your customers without any words."

_____

_____

_____

_____

I had you do this exercise because I wanted you to think about the businesses' names or logos that stand out to you the most and why. They somehow managed to grab your attention and by doing so made you remember them impulsively.

"You want to grab your customers' attention and have them remember you by impulse."

Now consider the exercise and answer the following questions.

You can always come back to this if you are not 100% sure about your answers.

Do you want your company to be recognized by your logo, your business name and logo, or just your business name?

_____

What colors would you like your business name or logo to be?

_____

Do you want your logo to be separated from your business name?

An example would be Target.

Do you want your logo to be attached to or within your business name?

An example would be Amazon. **amazon**.com

On the other hand, would you prefer your logo to be your business name?

An example would be Facebook. **facebook**.

Answer here:

_____

Note: *Before deciding, you can have a graphic designer produce each one so you can choose after seeing your options.*

Slogans

A slogan is generally used to let your customers know in a few words or sentences what you offer, an overview of your business, or what customers can expect from working with you.

Slogans are a great way to briefly speak to your customers and grab their attention. They are usually put underneath or on top of the business name. Your slogan should be displayed along with your business name as much as possible.

Examples:

IHOP—"Everything you (love) about breakfast"

The Home Depot—"More saving. More doing."

Martha's Wedding Decorations—"Elegance & Beauty, for your Special Day"

Just Right Outdoor Products—"Experience the outdoors like the PROS do"

Electro-Products—"Your electronics, keyboard, and hard drives supplier."

Once you have been in business for a while and built a customer base, you can change your slogan from listing your products or services to something more fun like –

Electro Products "We giga-byte our customers!"

Slogans are a great way to briefly speak to your customers and grab their attention.

With that being said, here is your task.

INTERACTIVE If you chose to use a slogan, write down a few examples that would work with your business. I would suggest to start out with listing what your business offers if it is not already in your business name. Slogans are usually changed more often than logos.

_____

_____

_____

_____

Now, choose the one slogan you wish to use and it will serve as your slogan for now.

Final Advice

If you choose to use a logo and/or slogan, make sure to include them every time your business name is displayed. Make sure your logo reflects either your industry, customer base and is something your customers can relate to. Let your slogan be easy enough to remember, informative enough to let your customers know what you offer and catchy enough to put a smile on their face.

Chapter 12

Business Hours, Company Policies & Agreements

"Developing your business structure and making it work."

Having your business hours, company policies & agreements in place before opening day will provide direction while operating your business. You will have a set time to provide customers with your products and services and they will know when to expect interaction with your business. You will also have set policies & agreements in place to refer to when dealing with any situations that may arise concerning your products or services.

 *Note: Whatever you decide in this chapter may change once you are actually in operation. There will be different things come up that you may not have thought about in the beginning. Do not worry about every single detail and treat it as a work-in-progress that changes over time.*

Example: When you have employees, you will need to factor in vacation time, holiday pay, pregnancy leave, sick time, death in the family time off, etc.

No need worrying about those things right now. Get the basics down and adjust your hours and policies as your business progresses.

Business Hours

Fitting a New Business into Your Current Schedule

One thing that you need to know is that your normal everyday schedule is about to change. Determining how much time you are able to invest into running your business depends upon your availability. You may want to think about letting go of some things you normally do for now. In this way, you can focus more time, attention, and energy on your new business.

More than likely, you are in one of these categories.

First Category - *You have a normal day job and want to start a business on the side. You will either continue operating your business part-time or eventually quit your day job to run your business full time. (This was my category)*

Second Category - *You do not have a normal day job and are able to focus 100% of your time and energy into running your business.*

First Category

This is probably going to be the most common category. I was grouped in this category when I first started in business.

First, let's write your work schedule. If you do not have a set work schedule, then write down what your schedule could look like in a normal workweek.

_____

_____

Next, determine the hours outside of your normal work schedule that you can commit to your new business.

Here is an example of what I did. Do not feel you need to follow this schedule by any means. We all have different schedules, circumstances, and priorities.

 *Remember, stay focused, follow a plan, and be confident that you can follow through. Just the fact that you are reading this book tells me that you can. I have the utmost confidence that you can accomplish your goals.*

My example: My work schedule was 7am – 4:30pm Mon-Fri.

 Every morning before work, I spent at least 30 minutes planning my next business move. During lunch, I placed phone calls, set appointments, and made connections. After my regular workday ended, I would work on my business until around 9:30pm (Sometimes until 11pm). On Saturday, I worked on my business from 9am-3pm. Afterwards I took the rest of Saturday and all day Sunday off.

Developing a set schedule assists you in forming a habit of knowing when you should be working on your business and helps you stay on track and focused.

Write down a general idea of the hours you are willing to put towards your business. If your regular work schedule permits, I would suggest you focus on operating your business the same hours your customers are available to do business with you. If you work evenings, you can use the morning and afternoon to run your business or vice versa. If you do not have a set schedule then planning the hours you will work on your business may be more challenging as you will need to adjust them regularly, then again no one said business would be easy.

_____

_____

_____

117

Another option is finding someone to run your business for you during the time you are working at your day job. That someone may be your spouse or significant other, hourly or commissioned employees or business partners. Be sure you can fully trust them to operate your business in your absence.

I have found it very helpful to commit to a schedule for running your business. It  *helps you stay on track and focused.*

Second Category

If you fall in this category, you are able to focus all your time, attention, and energy on starting your new business.

Your type of business will help determine the set hours you need to operate.

Example: If your business targets the public, you should try to be "open for business" the hours your customers are available.

If you were running a restaurant, you would definitely want to be open during lunch & dinner hours. However, if your restaurant were inside an office building or in an area full of office buildings, you would probably want to be open for breakfast and lunch.

If your business targets other businesses, you would want to be open during the hours the majority of your clients are open.

Write down the hours your customers are most likely available to do business with you.

_____

_____

_____

It would be in your best interest to use these hours when operating your business.

 Tip: Consider your daily schedule and adjust anything if necessary to help focus on running your business.

 On a Personal Note,

I suggest that you never put business before your family (loved ones).

In reality, business will always be there and there will constantly be something for you to work on, something to promote or more phone calls to make. You will never be able to get back the time that could have been spent with loved ones. No one on their deathbed ever wishes they had worked more. So make time for business but also make time for family (loved ones).

Company Policies & Agreements

Here you decide the rules of your company, how you choose to operate, make sales, initiate refunds, communicate to unsatisfied customers, and so forth.

It is very important to write out your company policies & agreements before starting your business. Please keep in mind that as you operate your business, your policies & agreements may change. Think of it as the rules you are setting for your company to abide by.

119

There are a few types of Company Policies & Agreements.

Three different types are:

1. The policies & agreements your company and employees follow.

2. The policies & agreements you share with your customers/clients.

3. The policies & agreements with your suppliers concerning your orders.

Let's start with the first one.

The Policies & Agreements Your Company and Employees Follow

(Employee policies will also be covered in Chapter 19 titled, "Hiring Employees")

> *Policies are guidelines on how to operate your business and what you expect from your employees.*

They serve as a written manual for reference in situations that may arise.

Examples:

1. You may want a written policy on operating with integrity, honesty, and fairness.

2. You may want a policy about no cursing, yelling, etc.

3. Most stores have a no shoes no shirt no service policy. (I guess no one cares about the pants.)

4. Your policy can include your operational hours and days your business is open.

5. It can include a dress code, a non-discrimination policy in the workplace, and a standard of operating in a professional manner.

6. It should include a non-disclosure agreement for your employees. A non-disclosure

is an agreement that your employee will not release any information about the inner workings of your company and its operations.

7. It should include a non-competition agreement. A non-competition agreement advises your employees that they cannot operate the same type of business for a specific number of years after their employment has ended. Without signing the agreement, they would be able to operate the same type of business and could possibly turn into your competition.

8. I would suggest including a statement advising your employees not to engage in any outside business activity that involves selling similar products or services.

For a complete list of general policies & agreements visit your local office-supply store and purchase a business document CD that includes policies & agreements.

Once you download it, you can edit the information to fit your business.

The Policies & Agreements You Share with Your Customers/Clients

The Policies & Agreements you share with your customers/clients will differ depending on your business type. Here are a few generic examples to consider when you are making decisions.

 *Note: Do not rely on a verbal agreement on any business transaction with your customers.*

It is always recommended that an agreement of any sort be in writing and preferably signed with a copy given to your customers (Signing is optional but helpful in disputes).

If you look at the back of your receipt when you purchase an item, you might find their store return or exchange policy. By purchasing the item, you automatically agree to their policy, whether you realize it or not. If your business transacts with other businesses, it is strongly suggested you give your clients a copy of your policies & agreements.

Here are a few things to think about when developing the policies & agreements you share with your customers or clients.

1. Do you want the sale of your product or service to be final? Meaning there are no exchanges or refunds.

2. Do you find refunds acceptable, as long as they are within a specific amount of time or brought back in perfect unused condition?

3. Will your policies & agreements be printed on the back of receipts, emailed, or printed and handed to your customers? Will you have your customers sign your policy or agreement? If you are a website company, typically you have a check box that customers can click that signifies agreement to your policies & agreements.

4. If you provide a product or service that does not require payment up front but does require payment after the product or service is completed or delivered; you may want your customers to sign an agreement stating they will pay within an authorized amount of time.

5. What happens if your customer does not pay on time?

6. For services, you want to document in exact detail what you are providing for the customer/client and compose your document to read precisely what the customer/client should expect along with an agreed-upon completion time.

7. Document in writing what your business is and is not liable for.

8. Remember to be fair when writing out your policies & agreements. Think about the times you were unhappy about a product or service and how you were treated. Were the companies' policies fair and how was your issue resolved?

9. Remember a happy customer is a repeat and referring customer.

This is not a comprehensive list as it will be up to you to write the details and cover as much information as possible for your policies & agreements. Keep in mind that the information you write today may change, be added to, or deleted over time.

For examples of policies & agreements, do an Internet search or you may pick up a business document CD at your local business supply store and edit the documents to fit your specific business.

Some businesses prefer to have an attorney write their policies & agreements. Depending on your budget, that may be an option you choose to consider as well.

Know Your Suppliers' Policies & Agreements

(Any businesses that you make purchases from)

So many different situations could arise from the moment you place an order to it being delivered at your door. It is extremely important to understand your suppliers' policies & agreements before placing any orders.

- What happens if the shipment arrives damaged?

- What if your order is incomplete?

- What happens if you get overcharged?

- What happens if the delivery company loses your shipment?

- If you are buying items to sell to your customers, are you able to return any items that did not sell?

- Is there a re-stocking fee for products?

- Does your supplier offer discounted or free shipping on certain quantity amounts?

These questions and others should be asked and their policies & agreements should be given to you in writing.

Take a moment and think of the different questions you will need answers for when it comes to ordering from your suppliers or making purchases for your company. The questions will be dependent upon your business type. Make sure to have an idea of the type of answers you would like to receive, as it will help you in deciding which suppliers or businesses to purchase from.

INTERACTIVE   List them here:

_____

_____

_____

_____

_____

_____

_____

It is rare for a company to operate and not have anything go wrong. Making sure the right agreements are in place is a very important factor, when operating your business. Not doing so can be very costly.

Write Your Policies & Agreements

Take this time to develop and write a few policies & agreements. Take your time, think carefully, and remember you can come back to this later; even so, it is highly recommended you do this before you begin operating your business. If you need assistance, I suggest using the document CD from an office supply store and editing the existing documents.

1. The policies & agreements your company and employees follow.

2. The policies & agreements you share with your customers/clients.

3. Usually suppliers will send you their policies & agreements. Read them thoroughly and respond with any modifications or additions if theirs lacks any specific details.

_____

_____

_____

_____

_____

_____

_____

_____

_____

_____

_____

_____

_____

_____

_____

_____

_____

_____

_____

_____

Final Advice

Always keep your policies & agreements updated. Make sure your employees and customers have access to them. Have them sign and date when necessary.

You are the business owner and will have the final authority on when to enforce or adjust your policies & agreements.

"I have found it very helpful to commit to a schedule for running your business. It helps you stay on track and focused."

Chapter 13

Business Plans

"Designing your road-map for success"

A business plan is a written document describing the nature of the business, the sales and marketing strategy, the financial background, and should contain a projected profit and loss statement.

Extremely **IMPORTANT** → Writing a business plan is required if you are going to need any type of funding.

If you are not going to need funding, I still suggest writing a business plan so you can have a basic road map to provide your business with direction, marketing strategies, sales process, and get a realistic idea of your expenses, etc.

Some may think a business plan is unnecessary. Let me ask you a question. If you were going to take a month-long trip to Europe for the very first time, would you just show up and see what happens or would you do some planning?

I hope you would do some planning and if so, why not take some time to write a plan for your new business venture, see the whole picture of your business, and hopefully avoid some common mistakes. Ultimately, you will have your business for much longer than a month's trip to Europe.

Realistically, no one can see into the future and determine every single step forward. However, it is still a good idea to have a business plan so you can have as much detailed information as possible.

If you need funding (money to start or operate your business) from a bank, business partner, investor, or any other source, you definitely need a business plan so you can present your ideas, plans, and strategies to the organization or person from which you are trying to obtain funding.

Business plans vary, so I will explain some of the generic details your plan should incorporate.

Generic Business Plan Details

Your business plan should be enclosed within a binder that allows you to slide a cover sheet in the front. Your cover sheet should list your business name, the names of all the owners, the company address, and phone number. If you have a logo, email address, or a website that should be included as well.

The titled pages should reflect the topics as follows:

The first page should have the same information as the cover page.

"Table of Contents" - this page depicts the enclosed topics and page numbers.

"Statement of Purpose" - Write out your business concept, your sales and profits for the current year (or expected sales and profits), and whether you have any patents or copyrights that apply to your products. Finally, your "Statement of Purpose" should be no more than a half page long with very direct points.

"Business Description" - This page can be a few paragraphs to a few pages depending on the complexity of your business. List the name of the business, entity type, and write a brief summary about your business industry. Provide details of how your industry is doing now and how it is projected to do in the near future. List your business category type (wholesale, retail, manufacture, food service, medical, restaurant, phone supplies, medical supplies for diabetes patients, etc.). Additionally, list the owners of the business and key personnel (this may just be yourself) along with everyone's knowledge or experience in the industry.

"Description of Products and Services" - When writing about your products and services be very clear as to what they are, what your costs are, how much you sell them for, and how your products or services are being used by your customers. Convey why you chose to sell your products or services and list how the loan or investment will be used to benefit the company. Example: If you need funding to fulfill orders. List your current and future suppliers. Add any significant contacts you have made that stimulate value to your business plan.

"Market Analysis" - Here you will list your "target market"; the type of customers most likely to purchase your product or service and state whether your sales are recurring or one-time purchases.

Example: An insurance company will make recurring sales while an auto dealership is a one-time purchase.

List your competitors pricing along with the strategies (marketing or sales) you plan to use to compete with them. Make sure to list your short and long-term strategies. Afterwards, list how you will market your products and services. This should include all advertising methods (Read Chapter 21 titled, "Advertising & Marketing" for a reference).

Last, list your distribution methods and describe in detail from the beginning to the end, of how you will get your products into the hands of your customers or provide your services. Start with where you procure your products; proceed to your process of selling the products/services to your customers, and how and when your customers receive it.

"Operations Management" - List how your business functions and what tasks or responsibilities are assigned to which division or personnel. Example: You may have a sales department, marketing & advertising department, accounting department, etc. If you will be taking on all these responsibilities yourself. Write how your business functions and describe how you are able to handle all the tasks needed to operate your business.

"Financial Statements" (**Your final main titled page**) - Here you will have three different types of financial statements.

1. Income statement
2. Cash flow statement
3. Balance sheet

An **Income Statement** shows your initial capital investment (how much of your own money you put into your business), how much money your company makes, what your expenses are, and "cost of goods" which is how much it cost you to purchase and/or produce the products you sell. See Chapter 30 titled, "Taxes, Expenses, and Business Insurance" for a list of general expenses your business may incur.

A **Cash Flow Statement** operates similar to your checkbook register. List your current income and actual expenses in addition to listing your future expenses. Expenditures like business loan payments, auto payments, equipment rentals, lease rental payments, etc., and when they are expected to be paid.

The statement looks ahead and shows you how much money you will need now and in the near future. You will carry over income and expenses from one month to the next. By doing this you eventually determine a reasonable estimate regarding how much it costs to operate your business.

It answers the questions:

• Where the money came (will come) from?

• Where it went (will go)?

Last is the **Balance Sheet**, which is used to calculate the net worth of a business.

It includes assets, liabilities, and equity.

Your assets are cash on hand, any type of equipment the business owns, tools, etc.

Liabilities are obligations that your company owes.

Owners' Equity is the amount of funds contributed by the owners plus the retained earnings (or losses).

For examples of balance sheets, income and cash flow statements, you can do an Internet search and add your business type. Example: cash flow statement for _____ (add your business type)

Keep in mind that depending on your industry and business type you may need to add a few more topics.

Submitting Your Business Plan

You will generally submit your business plan to:

1. A bank or financial institution, or an SBA office.

2. A business partner to join your business venture, which should require an initial investment on their part or expert knowledge and experience in the industry. It will also require you to hand over a percentage of the company which is called "equity."

3. An investor who will invest their money in your business venture. They may require equity but may also require royalties (commissions on every item sold), quarterly percentage distributions (a specific payout amount every three months), and/or a loan pay back plan.

 *Note: The difference between a business partner and an investor is a business partner will work with you and on the day-to-day operations. Partnerships usually have equal amounts of money invested into the business and share equally in risks.*

An investor will invest money and share industry knowledge, contacts and almost never work in day-to-day operations unless it is specified within the deal.

Note: Working with business partners and investors is also covered in Chapter 14 titled, "Funding Your Business" and Chapter 18 "Partnering With Others."

Bank, Financial Institution or SBA - Determine exactly how much you want to borrow, whether it is $5,000, $15,000, or $150,000. Write an explanation of how you will pay it back, and how long it will take you. If you have any type of collateral, (something that is pledged as security for repayment of a loan, it could be a house, car, etc.) you will want to write it down as well. Explain in detail exactly what you will do with the money, whether it is for equipment, products, etc.

Tips and Steps:

1. Set an appointment. Be on time and ready.

2. Bring your business plan. Be clear and confident when discussing your business.

3. Be ready to answer questions about your past experience, knowledge, projected sales and how you will make those sales.

4. Be convincing.

5. Your credit may be a determining factor so make sure it is in order.

Business Partner - For a business partner, write a summary of how much money you need them to invest along with what you expect from them. It could be a specific commitment on projects, day-to-day operations, or management over certain areas of your business. Additionally, list the amount of equity (percentage of your company) you are willing to hand over to them for partnering with you. Keep in mind that although it is highly suggested to require a cash investment, some business partners may bring with them industry "know-how" from years of experience that could be far more valuable than upfront cash. Make sure to explain in detail what you plan to do with the money the partner invests, whether it is for equipment, products, etc.

Tips and Steps:

1. Choose a partner you get along with.

2. Make sure they are experienced, passionate, and knowledgeable in your industry.

3. Make sure you both agree on the same vision for the company and have each job duties and expectations in writing.

4. Choose a partner you get along with. (Repeated on purpose)

Investors – When submitting a business plan to an investor, keep in mind that for you to be considered you most likely need to have ample knowledge and years of experience in the industry. Investors want to know current sales, projected sales and your plan to accomplish the sales. They will also want to know your current cash flow, cost of your products and services, what you sell them for, and your competitors prices.

Investors want to know how much money you want them to invest along with a plan on how they will get a return on their investment. They may also ask for equity (an ownership percentage) in your company in exchange for their investment. Make sure to explain in detail exactly what you will do with the money, whether it will be for equipment, bills, products, etc.

Investors usually never work on day to day operations, although they can be extremely valuable for your business as they bring the upfront cash you need, and may have industry knowledge along with business contacts. They believe in you, your idea, and your company. They are on board for you to succeed because your success means their investment is a success as well.

On a Personal Note,

Aside from the business plan you submit for funding, I advise you to develop a plan and strategy, which includes how to gain customers and retain them as repeat business (if your business is a repeat business). Then propose a strategy to scale (grow) your business when it is appropriate. Make sure you are able to sell your products and services 24/7 (functional website) and deliver exceptional customer service. I also recommend a referral program to reward your customers for referring others.

Have a plan A, plan B, and a Plan C. Make sure your strategy has several options to choose from in the event one does not work out.

Final Advice

Business plans may seem like a lot to write at first, especially if you are new to business. There are numerous resources to assist you in creating a business plan.

You can find samples of business plans by doing an Internet search for "business plans _____ (insert your industry). Then follow their guidelines, line by line to fit your specific business type.

You can go to a business supply store and buy a CD that has business plan templates, and you can edit a template, thus develop a business plan specified to your company.

You can also hire an accountant or CPA to do the business plan for you.

Chapter 14

Funding Your Business

"The process and options when financing your business"

Before applying for funding, you will need to have a general idea of how much it will cost to get your business started and running. If you are an existing business owner, you should have an idea of how much you need to stay operational, grow your business, or expand to more locations.

There are start-up costs which include business registration, rental deposits, equipment, logo and other graphic designs, website designs, licensing and permits, etc.

There are monthly costs which include monthly rental fee, office supplies, products that you sell, etc.

Start-Up Costs & Monthly Expenses

List the different types of costs you will have when starting and operating your business. I listed a few generic costs and common expenses. List other expenses according to your specific business.

- DBA, LLC, or Inc. Registration

- Graphic design for logo, advertisements, business cards, letterhead, envelopes, etc.

- Advertising materials – business cards, brochures, etc.

- Licensing & Permits.

- Office space, kiosk, retail location, warehouse, etc.

- Utility Services - most office buildings include utilities within your monthly rental fee. Retail locations generally do not.

- Phone line, fax line, and Internet.

- General office supplies and business equipment costs.

- Costs associated with the purchase of products you are selling.

- Website registration, hosting, and development.

- Signage costs (for retail and warehouse locations)

- Transportation costs

INTERACTIVE List any other additional costs that you can think of for your business. The final number may not be exact but will give you a good general idea of how much funding you will need.

_____

_____

_____

_____

_____

_____

_____

_____

_____

_____

_____

Funding Options

When it comes to funding your business here are a few choices.

- Using your own money to invest in your business.

- Asking a bank or other lending institution to borrow money.

- Asking family/friends to borrow money.

- Finding an Investor or Business Partner.

- Small Business Administration.

- Choosing lower cost options.

- Crowdfunding, which are websites that help raise funds for start-ups.

Here are the details about each choice.

Using your own money to invest in your business

Investing your own money means, you owe no one and you start your business without any debt. Many business owners have used savings, 401k's, or their income tax refunds to start a business.

Asking a bank or other lending institution to borrow money

Using a bank to apply for a small-business loan <u>will require a business plan</u>. The bank assumes the risk of loaning the money and requires your personal financial statements, including tax returns. If you are a new business, they will look at your personal credit history as well as your current source of income. If you are an existing business, they will look at your business financial statements and tax returns and still may require your personal financial information. The bank may ask for collateral equal to 20% to 30% of the loan amount.

There are several loan and finance companies operating independently from banks. They may provide you a business loan based on certain criteria like your credit score, your debt to income ratio, bank statements, and/or collateral (something with value you use as surety for payment of a debt). Some collateral loans will be from 40% to 75% of your collateral value.

I suggest you start at your local bank, then try a few other financial associations for a clear understanding of what is required of you and weigh your options. If you want to obtain funding by a loan company, do an online search for "loan companies" or "loan for my business" to find some funding options.

Finally, using a bank or loan company will not require you to give up equity in your business (share a percentage of company ownership).

Asking family or friends to borrow money

Some of us have been born into a family that has the generous "rich uncle" and some of us have been born into a family with the "weird uncle." If you borrow from family or friends, they are likely basing their decision on your business idea, plan, execution, and character; since, they have known you for years. They may want a percentage of the business, some type of collateral, or a payback with interest plan.

If your business succeeds your bond may be strengthened. If the business fails it could lead to "close to home" issues if you are not able to pay back the loan. You may lose a friend, be harassed or ignored by family member(s); in some cases, your debt may be forgiven. I would advise you to consider alternate options before using this one, unless your family member or friend is going to share ownership and assume some of the risk, or you guarantee a loan payback over time.

Investor or Business Partner

Having an investor, or a business partner are worthwhile options for your new business. You may need to negotiate before coming to an acceptable agreement of who will be responsible for what and dividing ownership, if applicable. When working with investors, you will definitely need a business plan and have experience or knowledge in the industry. Most investors prefer your business to be in operation and show a steady increase in sales.

An investor or business partner will want to know:

- Your level of knowledge and experience in your field of business.

- If your idea is proprietary (exclusively owned by trademark or patent) or could be copied by someone else.

- Your pricing and your competitors pricing.

- How you are marketing your products or services.

- How many customers or repeat customers you have.

- How your business is different from similar businesses.

143

- What do you plan to do with the money.

- That you are passionate about your business and willing to work hard to see it become successful.

- What responsibilities they will take on as a partner.

 They may glance at your business plan, set it down and speak directly to you so be ready to answer questions about your business and business plan.

Although most investors prefer your business to be in operation, some investors and partners are interested and willing to invest in the initial start-up phase. You will need to explain in detail how your business idea works. Understand that an investor or partner trusts you with his or her own money. They believe that you and your idea will work without any actual sales. Remember, just because you think your business idea is the best idea in the world does not mean an investor or potential business partner will. Your job is to convince them.

If you and a partner came up with the idea and business plan yourselves, you would normally split everything down the middle at 50% each. Regardless of the percentage split, be sure to write out all roles and responsibilities and determine who will be in charge of what.

You and an investor can work multiple ways on a deal. Before receiving any funding, you and the investor must come to an agreement and document it in writing with both of your signatures.

Keep in mind that terms are always negotiable *before* signing.

Whether your business is a new start-up or an existing business; if you are working with an investor or partner, you may be asked to give up some equity (percentage of ownership in your business) or guarantee a return on investment. Example: If an investor gave $8000, then they would receive $8000 back plus an agreed upon amount within a specific time frame.

 *Note: Whoever owns 51% or more takes control of the company.*

An investor or partner may require participation in essential business decisions, which can be granted dependent on their percentage of ownership and the agreement you entered with them. This might not be a bad idea if they have years of business experience, industry knowledge, valuable contacts, and are interested in a prosperous result with their investments, just as I am sure you are.

In some cases, working with an investor or partner may be particularly beneficial if everyone comes to terms with a satisfactory agreement. I look at investors and partners with this mindset. If they bring funding while adding value as in industry know-how, experience, and valuable contacts, perhaps using an investor or partner would be well worth it.

I could sell 1,000 products on my own and keep all the profits myself, or sell 10,000 products with the help of an investor or partner and keep half of the profits, which should I choose? It only makes sense to go with an investor or partner since I end up making more sales and profits at the end of the day. If an investor or partner cannot add value, you may consider getting a bank loan and keeping your equity or offering a guaranteed return on investment plus an agreed upon amount.

Finally, an investor will also want to know:

A. **Total Sales** – is a total of all sales made from all outlets you own unless asked to have total sales broken down by each location or source. An example of a source could be total sales from in store, total sales from online, etc. Total sales could also be broken down to months, quarterly, or yearly.

B. **Net Profits** - is your total sales dollars remaining after deducting expenses.

C. **Business Valuation** – is the process of determining the economic value of a business or company (the total dollar value of your business).

Working with a partner will be explained in further detail in Chapter 18 titled, "Partnering with Others."

Small Business Administration–SBA provides loans to businesses; so the requirements of eligibility are based on specific aspects of the business and its principals. As such, the key factors of eligibility are based on what the business does to receive its income, the character of its ownership and where the business operates.

SBA generally does not specify what businesses are eligible. Rather, the agency outlines what businesses are not eligible. However, there are some universally applicable requirements. To be eligible for assistance, businesses must:

- Operate for profit.

- Be small, as defined by SBA.

- Be engaged in, or propose to do business in, the United States or its possessions.

- Have reasonable invested equity.

- Use alternative financial resources, including personal assets, before seeking financial assistance.

- Be able to demonstrate a need for the loan proceeds.

- Use the funds for a sound business purpose.

- Not be delinquent on any existing debt obligations to the U.S. government. (SBA)

Choosing Lower Cost Options–Depending on the type of business you decide to start will determine whether there are lower cost options available. For instance, you may consider working from home instead of an office until you make enough money for an office. You could meet your clients at their office, local restaurants, or coffee shops with Internet access. Not all business is conducted from an office. Several business owners work from home until it is necessary to move into an office.

If your business requires office space, perhaps you can sub-lease a room from an existing business or ask the office building manager if they offer smaller one-room offices for lease.

If your business requires retail space, perhaps you could look into setting up a kiosk in a mall, area shopping centers, or inside an existing store. In this way, you could build a customer base without the major expense of a retail space up front.

Here are three ideas to lower cost and expenses in the early stages of starting your business. Not all business types are listed so learn from the examples and identify which lower cost options are available to you.

- Instead of opening a full service gym, maybe offer outside exercise classes at a park or lease a room at a community center.

- Instead of opening a restaurant, start out with a food truck or a catering service.

- Instead of opening a retail store, you can use a kiosk, start an online store, or consider using websites like ebay.com to sell your products.

The key is to find alternative ways to build your customer base without large upfront costs. Your business needs customers to make sales; without sales, there is no business. If your expenses outweigh your profits, there is no business.

Crowdfunding – This option has recently been made available thanks to truly innovative people who had an idea to give new businesses a platform to raise start-up capital. Crowdfunding enables you to receive monetary support from people; who in turn are able to receive products at reduced rates, package deals, or pre-release products (released earlier than the general publics date). A couple of websites you can view for more information are www.KickStarter.com and www.indiegogo.com. Search the Internet for crowd funding to find other available options.

Note: This type of funding is not for all types of businesses.

Final Advice

If I had to place the options explained in this chapter in order, I would highly suggest using your own money.

If that were impracticable, I would consider using lower cost options, finding a business partner or looking for an investor. If your business idea is unique enough and caters to the public, choosing "crowd funding" might be a great option for you. Finally, I would choose a bank loan as the last option.

Chapter 15

How and Where to get the Products You want to Sell

"If you are in the product business then this is the right chapter for you!"

Manufacturing

A manufacturing company is a business that actually fabricates or constructs products. Ordinarily, they are not set up to sell directly to the public, although some manufacturers do, they usually sell finished products direct to other businesses. There are several manufacturers here in the US and numerous enterprises globally. Most manufacturing companies require businesses to place large quantity orders for products to be produced.

 *Note: Provided your business type is manufacturing, you will need to find sources that procure raw materials and equipment necessary to fabricate your products.*

Wholesale

A wholesale company is usually a business who buys in large quantities from manufacturers and sells them in smaller quantities to businesses. They charge more per item than the manufacturing company charges, but in general, they do not require particularly large orders. They may offer a variety of selections on orders including multiple colors, lower minimums, and a varied selection of styles.

Finding Your Products

Research will be required to find suppliers for your desired products. You will have to decide between purchasing from a manufacturer or a wholesaler. A manufacturing company generally offers products at a lower-cost rate than wholesalers, while requiring you to buy in bulk. It is best to check with them directly. A few manufacturers allow small quantity purchases.

If the manufacturer does not allow you to buy in smaller quantities, and you are not financially able to buy in bulk; a wholesale company may be a better option.

 *Note: You usually will need a <u>Sales Tax Permit</u> in order to purchase from U.S. wholesalers and manufacturers.*

Internet Search

To locate a manufacturing company or a wholesale company you simply search the Internet for "_____ (list your product) manufacturing" or "_____ (list your product) wholesale." You may find several companies that come up. Call or inspect their website to see if they truly are a manufacturing or wholesale company.

To verify if a business is wholesale, ask them if they sell directly to the public or only to businesses. If they sell exclusively to businesses, they are a wholesale company. If they sell to the public, advise them you have a sales tax permit and ask what your price will be for quantity orders (buying more than one of the same items). If they offer price reductions, they qualify as a wholesale company. However, if they do not require a copy of your sales tax permit or offer a price reduction for quantity orders, they are not a wholesale company.

The only way to know if a business is a viable manufacturer is to ask them if they actually "manufacture" their own products either locally or abroad. If they answer yes, you are speaking to a manufacturer. If the answer is no, and they in fact, receive products from a supplier; you are not dealing with a manufacturer.

Once you have located a few manufacturing or wholesale companies, call or visit them and ask to set up an account to resell their products. These companies may require your sales tax permit information, so make sure to have it handy. In addition, a few companies may require that you have an established retail location or an online store before buying products for resale.

Public or Online Store

Another way to locate products you want to sell is by visiting a public or online store. Look to see if the manufacturer or wholesaler is listed anywhere on the product packaging or description. If so, contact the company for pricing and quantity requirements.

Trade Shows (Also covered in Chapter 21 titled, "Advertising & Marketing")

Instead of visiting vendors throughout the country, you can visit a number of them at Trade Shows for your industry type. This way, you can communicate effectively with several companies with one visit.

Trade shows are frequently hosted in major cities across America including Las Vegas, New York City, Los Angeles, and Dallas. These shows normally cater to a variety of business industries. Research and see which Trade Shows cater to your specific business type or industry.

If your business is in manufacturing, distribution, or sells products and/or services to other businesses, you should learn when and where your industry Trade Show is taking place. Thus, you can inquire as to booth rentals for your company to display products and services.

At Trade Shows manufacturers, distributors, and retailers showcase their existing or future line of products to businesses or consumers.

It is a great way to connect and communicate with the businesses that provide products for your industry type. As a retailer, you can view merchandise, negotiate, and place orders for products that you wish to sell.

Usually the products offered at Trade Shows are going to be available for the next season or become available within a manufacturing time frame. For some Trade Shows it is necessary to submit proof that you are in the industry before you can attend. **It is best to check with the organizers directly for their specific requirements and determine if the trade show will exhibit what you are looking for.**

To determine when and where trade shows in your industry will be taking place; search the Internet for "trade shows _____ (list your business type or industry). The information you need is made available on the search results. Just remember, travel may be required so make sure you factor that into your budget.

Payment Options

Payment terms are either credit or prepay.

Credit – As a small business owner you are able to apply for credit with your suppliers.

This is how it works:

A supplier will ask you for past references of businesses that have invoiced you and received payment within the allowed time, customarily within thirty days. They contact your references to verify you have a reliable history of paying your bills on time. Next, they determine the amounts you have paid and issue credit based on your payment history and invoiced amounts.

If your business is new, you probably do not have business references, thus you may have to buy on a prepaid basis for now. Once you have established a relationship with the supplier and have prepaid for a few months you can request for credit terms again.

Final Advice

I suggest researching periodically to see if you can save money on the purchase of your products. If you find a lower cost, communicate the amount to your current supplier, they may match the cost to keep your business.

Keep in mind when choosing suppliers that cheaper is not always better. Some businesses switch suppliers to save money, only to find out that what they use to get in one week ended up taking three weeks. The wait time is not worth the few dollars saved.

Chapter 16

Credit Card Processing for Your Business

"Today most people use credit or debit cards as their preferred method of payment"

Setting up your business for credit and debit card processing is in your best interest. Loss of sales is inevitable when customers do not have this as a payment option.

Step One— Determine your process

Determine if you want to process payments in person, over the phone, online or all three.

Step Two — Compare your options

In order to prepare your business for credit card processing you need to contact a merchant service provider (MSP). You will want to check with a few different MSPs and compare your fees and options.

 *Note: If you want to sell your products or services online you need an MSP, a shopping cart, a SSL Certificate and a payment gateway account.*

Step Three — Understanding your fees

There are different processing and monthly fees each merchant service provider charges. Make sure you get all fee information up front. Credit card fee rates vary and with certain companies, your fees depend on how much you actually process on a monthly basis.

Some MSPs will need to know what your products or services cost and an estimate of how much your anticipated sales will be by credit or debit cards before assigning a fee structure. For instance, if you sold specialty candles on a website, conceivably each ticket could be around $25 to $40 dollars and all sales would be online. If you sold office furniture, your sales receipts might be $500 to $2,000 and 70% of customers might pay with credit or debit cards in person. There is no way to know definitely if your business is in start-up mode. So give your best estimate.

How Credit Card Fees Work

Every time you make a purchase with your debit or credit card you simply swipe, enter your pin, or sign, and you are on your way with your new merchandise. If the cost was $100, you will see a charge on your bank or credit card statement for $100. The business you purchased from receives (depending on their rate) approximately $96 to $98 dollars for the $100 purchase. The remaining amount goes towards paying credit card processing fees.

Some merchant service providers charge a swipe rate plus a transaction fee. Swipe rates can be anywhere from 1.63% to 3.67% and keyed-in rates could be 2.19% to 4.01% (for example only; actual fees may vary slightly) per each transaction your customer pays with a credit card. Typically, on top of that fee there is a transaction fee of around twenty-five cents. If a customer uses a debit card with a pin code, the rate fee may be lower than if the customer uses their card as a credit card.

Swipe is when a customer is present and they hand over the card or swipe it on a terminal themselves.

Keyed-in is when a customer or card is not present which usually occurs when allowing customers to pay over the phone for products or services.

All credit card processing companies charge varied fees for their services and they compete with their rates to win your business.

 Visit SmallBusinessAA.com for more information concerning Business Registration, Website Development & Online Store, Domain Name (website name), Business Email, Credit Card Processing, Graphic Design & Advertising Materials.

Final Advice

As a new business owner, you will get several offers from MSPs offering you credit card processing services. Do not concede to any sales person's aggressive tactics and allow them to pressure you into signing an agreement you are not 100% comfortable with.

Chapter 17

Choosing Your Business Location

"Location, Location, Location"

Your type of business determines the type of location that would be best suited for you and your customers.

Here are a few basic choices when deciding on a location for your business.

- Online (your location is the World Wide Web)

- Work from home

- Small, medium, or large office space

- Retail

    1. *Lease a kiosk in a mall or shopping center*

    2. *Lease a space inside of an existing retail store (sublease)*

    3. *Lease a store in a mall or a storefront shopping center*

    4. *Stand-alone retail location (good for restaurants and gas stations)*

- Storage facility with an office combination

- Warehouse facility

Online (your location is the World Wide Web)

If you are an online company, I suggest you have a fully functional website before launching your business:

1. Your homepage should be clear and concise. Not too cluttered. Visitors should be able to easily understand what you offer; to quickly locate the product or service for more information or to purchase.

2. Your website should be "search engine optimized" so potential customers can find your listing when searching for products or services on Internet search engines.

3. Make sure to have your customer service phone number displayed and hours of operation so customers are able to communicate with you if they need further assistance.

4. Have your terms and conditions as well as your refund policy on your site.

5. If your business is on social media, you should have links to your social media accounts on your site.

6. You should have a "sign up for email updates" link on your site to keep in touch with your site visitors.

7. Make sure your website has an SSL certificate if you are going to accept payments online.

8. You should have a few shipping options for customers to choose from.

9. I suggest selling your products on other nationally or globally recognized websites like Amazon.com and ebay.com, etc. By doing this, you are placing your products in front of potential customers that would rarely know of your company's existence.

Work From Home

If your business allows you to work from home make sure you have a dedicated area (example: garage) and hours you work. There needs to be a level of self-discipline on your part because the option of sleeping in or watching TV could be tempting for some.

Be sure you take advantage of the tax deduction allowed for using part of your home as a business expense and have insurance coverage for your inventory and equipment.

Small, Medium, or Large Office Space

For office professionals that sell to the public or other businesses, I suggest your location be in an office building near a major freeway or highway. It gives your clients added convenience when visiting your office and provides you quick access to commute for sales appointments.

Select an office that has just enough space for what you need to operate. Choosing a space larger than what you need will result in wasted space and money. If you anticipate growth early on, choose an office space that has an option for expansion. In most buildings, the management will build or knock down walls, change carpet or paint according to your specifications before you move in. Be sure to negotiate these options before signing.

If your business is aimed towards the local community for customers, I suggest acquiring a location in that community. Examples of businesses applying this method are insurance companies, hair salons, local restaurants, attorney's offices, and coffee or yogurt shops. They are located in and service the local community.

Retail

Kiosks are a great start for any retail business to showcase products in a mall or shopping center without having to pay the higher cost of monthly rental fees a traditional store would incur. Make sure you choose a mall or shopping center where your customers are most likely to shop. You will have a chance to test the demand for your products without signing a long lease or having to spend too much on upfront costs.

As customers walk by they can view your products with ease as items are displayed in an open setting. Typically, kiosks are rented on a month-to-month basis so there are no long term contracts to sign. You need to be creative in displaying your products as most kiosks come with a standard look so branding might be somewhat difficult. You are limited on space to stock inventory so you may need to restock often.

 Generally, during the winter holidays the monthly rental fee increases significantly, so make sure you budget accordingly. Display your top selling items at every possible angle, allowing potential customers quick views as you only get a few seconds to spark interest. Interest causes an inquiry and inquiries lead to sales, if the price is right. Lastly, the mall or shopping center may request a percentage fee based on your sales per month. No one likes paying fees; however, if you think of the store as partner, who gets a small percentage of sales and in return brings you plenty of customers. It makes sense.

Subleasing inside of an existing store can be beneficial as long as you and the store both share the same customer base. Usually the leasing requirements are month-to-month without deposits unless the existing store is doing some remodeling to accommodate your needs. I suggest an effective advertising campaign in your local area instead of relying on walk-in customers from the existing store. Utility costs are often included but may vary from store to store.

Leasing a store in a mall or a storefront shopping center is an option for businesses that have a proven demand and sales method for their products or services. You will need more capital to get started as you may be required to pay the first and last month's rent as well as a deposit (depending on the management's rules). Your lease term period could be anywhere from six months to three years.

Determine if racks, fixtures, and stands come with the space or if you need to purchase them yourself (if your business requires them). Find out if utilities are included in the monthly rent, or if you need to secure them yourself. Design your storefront appearance to make it inviting as well as intriguing. Customers want to see "Sale" signs and "20% off" signs, etc.

Make sure your business name signage and packaging are designed to attract the customers who are most likely to purchase from you. Finally, the mall or shopping center may request a percentage fee based on your sales per month. As stated earlier, no one likes paying fees; however, if you think of the store as a partner, who gets a small percentage of sales and in return brings you plenty of customers. It makes sense.

Standalone retail locations can be leased or built from the ground up. This option requires a significantly large financial investment. It should only be pursued once you have a proven business model.

Storage Facility with an Office Combination

If you live in a major city, there are plenty of storage facilities with offices to choose from. Many of these units provide a storage room for inventory, equipment, and a shipping station as well as an attached office for you to work out of. Storage facilities traditionally do not require a long-term commitment but rather a month-to-month "cancel anytime" lease.

If your business type permits it, this is a great alternative when your new business has outgrown your home garage.

In contrast, if you do not live in an immensely populated area, you will have to do some research to see what is available in your area.

Warehouse Facility

Ordinarily, businesses that sell products to other businesses use warehouse type locations to store inventory, package their products and ship to customers. This is similar to the storage with office option except warehouses are generally much larger and can hold more inventory. They normally include shipping docks for trucks to load and unload, and require a signed lease for a specific period, usually one to three years.

How to Find a Location for Your Business?

In general, you can do an Internet search for available office, retail, store, or warehouse space in your city. Additionally, most companies advertise their space for lease on signage outside of their property. Contact the property manager for details; they will want to know how much space you are looking for so make sure you have an idea of the square footage your business requires.

Requirements

Companies who lease space have different requirements; I have listed a few generic requirements although you will have to get specific information from the property manager.

- Your business registered with the county or state.

- Commercial insurance. They will need your business to be covered up to a specific amount (they will give you that amount) and may ask to be listed on your policy.

- Sign permit if you plan to hang any signage on their property.

- First and last month's rent or a deposit.

- Occupancy permit.

- For new businesses with no rental history, the property owners may need to see bank statements to prove you are able to pay the monthly rental fee.

Things to Know before You Sign

- Make sure you know what you are liable for.

  1. Utilities

  2. Maintenance

  3. Any property upkeep

- Is there a long-term contract you have to sign or is it a month-to-month rental?

- Make sure you understand that once you sign and agree to the lease terms that you are locked in for the length of the agreement. Since your business is new, the property management will ask you to guarantee the lease personally as well as your business. If you break that agreement, you will be personally liable for the remaining lease balance and that may affect your credit rating. You may ask for a clause in your lease that states, "With a 30 day written notice you may be released from your lease if you happen to close your business."

- Contracts can range anywhere from one to three years. Generally, the longer the term you are willing to sign for, the lower monthly cost.

- Know the required commercial insurance amounts.

- Know the hours of operation the property is open and make sure they line up with the hours you need to operate your business.

- If you feel that growth is in the near future you will want to make sure the property can accommodate your business needs without having to move locations. Typically, knocking down a few walls or utilizing extra space nearby can adapt to your growth depending on your business type.

- Customarily when you sign for more than one year, most property owners are willing to tailor the space to fit your needs. Find out if the property is willing to build or knock down walls, add new carpet, etc.

- For businesses that will service customers at their location. Is this location conveniently located and easily accessible?

 On a Personal Note,

If your business is "able to," (no need for customers to visit you) I would suggest working from home and saving on rental expenses. Once you start making profits you can gradually work your way to an office, storage or warehouse environment. If your business is in retail, obviously, you cannot do this although you can start online, lease a kiosk or small retail space, or sublease from another business.

When I stated, "able to," I am referring to business types that offer products or services typically to other businesses, your business is a website company, or a business that interacts with or makes sales directly to its customers at their location; therefore, there is no need for your customers to visit you.

Here is a list of businesses that started from home or a dorm room.

Amazon.com founded in 1994 by Jeff Bezos and started out of his garage. (Bezos)

Apple, Inc. founded in 1976 by Steve Jobs and Steve Wozniak and first ran the company out of a garage. (Jobs)

The Walt Disney Company founded by Walt and Roy Disney in 1923. Walt and Roy moved in with their uncle Robert and worked on their company out of his garage. (Disney)

Google.com founded in 1998 by Larry Page and Sergey Brin and started out of a garage. (Page)

Harley Davidson founded in 1903 by William S. Harley and Arthur Davidson and started out of a wooden shed. (Harley) (Davidson Sr.)

Dell Computer founded by Michael Dell in 1984 out of a dorm room. (Dell)

My point is for you to focus on your business and make sales. Solve problems for your customers by providing them with your products or services. If possible, grow gradually into leasing or buying space and save on that upfront expense.

Everyone's situation and preference is different so ultimately only you know what is best for your company, please choose wisely.

Consider Your Location Options

Let's take a moment, think about the location options for your business, and list them here.

_____

_____

_____

Research and call around for prices and find out what is required in order to gain approval for leasing a space.

Do not only get the monthly rate but also ask what they charge for "CAM charges" or "operating expenses." CAM charges are fees that all tenants pay (by sharing the cost) to keep the property functioning. It could range anywhere from water, to lawn care, to electricity and more. Some property managers will quote the lease amount and CAM together and some quote it separately, so make sure you ask. Cam stands for "Common Area Maintenance."

List the prices and requirements here.

_____

_____

_____

_____

_____

Ultimately, your final choice will be based on necessity, cost, and the amount of funds you have available to spend on rental fees.

Take your time and carefully consider your options before making a final decision.

Chapter 18

Partnering with Others

"Together we can accomplish more, sometimes"

Have you ever heard the saying "two minds are better than one"? Well in business, there is a chance that is true as long as you and your partner have the same vision and mission for the company. If not, you will find yourselves arguing more than accomplishing goals.

Role of a Business Partner

Partner by definition is a person associated with another or others as a principal or a contributor of capital in a business or a joint venture, customarily sharing its risks and profits. A partner is someone that is going to work side by side with you although usually in different areas within the same business. (Douglas Harper, Historian.)

A partner shares in responsibilities, risks, and profits.

Partners commonly bring with them industry experience and a capital investment (upfront cash) towards the business.

Example:

Let's say three people are partners in business and all agree with the vision and mission. Their duties and responsibilities should be according to their strengths.

Partner 1	Partner 2	Partner 3
Cash Investment	Cash Investment	Cash Investment
Sales	Accounting	Operations Management
Negotiating	Budgeting	Administration
Marketing	Pricing	Industry Experience
Advertising		

Investors can be viewed as partners if they are working in operations within the business as well as providing capital. However, some investors will only want to provide a capital investment and expect a return.

Owner	Investor/Partner	Investor Only
Cash Investment	Cash Investment	Cash Investment
Sales	Operations Management	
Negotiating	Industry Experience	
Marketing	Consulting	
Advertising	Business Connections	
Accounting	Distribution Channels	
Budgeting & Pricing		

Before going further I need to clearly state, " that partnerships are not for every business owner."

If you choose to work with a partner or partners, you must determine what percentage they will own of the business. That amount should be determined by their role in the company and capital investment.

If there are only two partners, most will do a 50/50 or a 49/51 split.

 *Note: Whoever owns more equity has more control of the company.*

Pros and Cons of Partnerships

Pros:

- More capital (cash) to invest.

- People with different backgrounds and experience are able to apply their expertise to their role in the company.

- Level of liability is evenly distributed.

- You would have another business professional to bounce back and forth new ideas.

- You could reach your target market (people who are most likely to purchase your product or service) at a faster and more progressive rate if partners are experienced in sales and marketing.

- You do not have to do everything yourself, partners can share the responsibilities of running the company.

Cons:

- As time progresses partners may not agree with the vision, mission, or direction the company is heading.

- Some partners may want more earnings because they feel they do more of the work and can cause disagreements.

- In some cases, businesses have encountered a huge problem because a partner spent unnecessarily or ran off with the profits.

- In some instances, your partners join to team-up against you and use their voting power to change things within the company. Let's say you own 40% and two other partners each own 30% of the company. The other two partners could join forces and vote for something you do not necessarily agree with; since their ownership-combined totals 60%, they have the final say.

Partnering by Offering Small Percentages of Your Company

Some business owners have chosen to offer small percentages of their company to key personnel they could not otherwise afford. For instance, let's say you want to start a wedding and event planning business because you are a great organizer and love putting designs together. You could hire a marketing professional and offer 5-12% of your company instead of a high salary. You would have the benefit of a marketing professional without giving up too much equity in your company. That principal can be applied to any business and works with key positions within your company.

Teaming up with other Businesses

Contact a company that offers products or services different from yours but you both service the same clients.

Example: Let's say your business is an accounting service, and the majority of your clients are small businesses.

Small businesses need printing, office furniture and equipment, as well as advertising services. If you were to contact local companies that offer those products or services and start referring your clients to them: they can in turn, start referring their clients to your accounting service. All parties would mutually benefit. Keep in mind that only brochures and business cards should be exchanged between your businesses, so they are available to hand out when a customer might need your product or service.

 Tip: Offer the Most Requested Services Yourself

You may also find that your business could offer more products or services, instead of referring customers to another company.

More will be explained on expanding your products and services in Chapter 24 titled, "Maximizing Your Business Potential."

Final Advice

Remember, that the decision to use a partner does not have to be immediate; you can add a partner at any time. Personally, I think it is a great opportunity, only if it is necessary to reach the specific goals you have for your company and your partner agrees with the vision, mission and goals of the company.

Acquiring a partner can be very helpful because someone else will care about the success of your business as much as you do.

If you have the capital, you could always hire someone to help run your company as a high-level employee. Pay them a salary without giving any equity, which means you still own 100% of your company.

If you do acquire a partner, make sure you cover every single detail in your contract or agreement.

Details could consist of:

1. Cash investment amount required

2. Equity amount each partner will receive

3. Job duties and responsibilities of each partner

4. If a disagreement occurs who has the final say so?

"Everyone's situation and preference is different so ultimately only you know what is best for your company, please choose wisely."

Chapter 19

Hiring Employees

"When is it time to hire and what is the hiring process?"

In order for your business to grow you must eventually hire or outsource help. Trying to manage it all by yourself could cause you to lose focus and therefore, decrease productivity.

Hiring in itself can be a challenging task. Your goal is to place someone in a position that you can no longer handle yourself. You will want their attitude, education, skills, and past experiences to line up with your job requirements.

> *"Hiring an employee means trusting and paying someone else to do the duties that you can no longer do alone."*

Your immediate cash flow or loan amount will determine whether you are able to hire employees at the onset of your business, unless you are paying them by commission. (Commissions are covered in this chapter)

When is it time to hire?

Several business owners choose to operate their business by themselves for the start-up phase through the first couple of years.

If this is you, here are a few examples of when it is time to start hiring employees.

- If you are not able to answer your business phone on a consistent basis because you are doing other business related activities. You are missing sales if you are not able to communicate with customers.

- If your customers are waiting too long for your products or services, as you are servicing other customers.

- If you want to expand your business to a second location, but your time is limited.

- If the customer demand for your product or service exceeds your ability to fulfill those orders because of time constraints.

- If you are stressing yourself to the point that operating your business is more of a burden due to the workload you have to handle.

These examples indicate your business is growing and you need help!

Growth is a great thing when operating any business but requires hiring and trusting employees.

Hiring Process

Hiring an employee means trusting and paying someone else to do the duties that you can no longer do alone.

You will need to train your employees for every job duty you assign them so they will know exactly how you want the job done.

Before choosing a hiring option make sure you determine the job title, description, requirements, method you will use to let the public know you are hiring and your budget.

Job Title, Description, and Requirements

Job Title - Bookkeeper, Secretary, Sales, General Labor, Tech Support, Engineer, and etc.

Job Description – Part-time, full-time, employee will be responsible for the following duties…

Requirements - Determine what requirements you are looking for in your candidates.

Examples would be:

- High School Graduate, College Hours or College Degree
- They Must Have Reliable Transportation
- Years of Experience
- No Experience Required But Offer Training
- Customer Service Oriented
- Management or Administrative Experience
- Sales or Marketing Experience
- Ability to Multi-Task, Etc.
- Flexibility with Scheduling

The lists of requirements depend on your business type, available positions, and what you as an employer, are looking for in a possible candidate. If you need help in writing a job posting, do an Internet search for "how to write a job posting" and go through the different links for examples.

U.S. Equal Employment Opportunity Commission

You also need to follow the guidelines set by the U.S. Equal Employment Opportunity Commission, which prohibits discrimination against race, color, religion, sex (including pregnancy), national origin, age (over 40), disability or genetic information. For more information, please visit   www.EEOC.gov. (Commission)

Where to Post Job Hiring Ads

If your business is a restaurant or retail business, you can post a "Now Hiring" sign out front so potential job candidates may inquire inside to apply.

If your business is not in a retail environment, you can post employment ads in the local papers distributed in the area. Jobs can be posted online and at employment websites too. (Examples: Monster.com, Craigslist.org, CareerBuilder.com just to name a few.) You may also contact your local unemployment office, or local colleges in the area and let them know you are an employer seeking to fulfill a job position.

Budget

Once you have determined the job title, job description, requirements and method of hiring, you should determine your budget allowance for the position's pay scale before posting any ads. Most companies offer hourly wages or salaries based on the size of their company, candidate's job duties, experience, and education.

You might want to consider staying competitive with other companies that are similar in size to yours and keep the wages within similar ranges for the same types of position and job descriptions. Not staying competitive could result in wasted time of hiring and training just to have your employee quit and go to work for another company, who pays more for the same type of work.

Hiring Options

You have a few hiring options to choose from:

- Hiring an hourly employee

- Hiring a salary employee

- Paying employees by commission

- Outsourcing

- Interns

- Volunteers

Hiring Hourly Employees

This means you will pay them a set hourly wage for every hour they work for your company. Be aware of your state's minimum wage laws. Compliance is mandatory; you do not want your employee's wage lower than the legal requirement. If your employee works more than 40 hours a week every hour over 40 will be considered overtime, and should be paid at the base rate plus (+) half base rate (if applicable in your state). For example, if you pay an employee $10 per hour, and they worked over 40 hours, then every hour over 40, the employee will be earning $15 per hour.

Hiring Salaried Employees

Salaried personnel are more common in higher-level positions. Even though, other position levels may be compensated as salaried employees as well.

Essentially, you pay them a set monthly or yearly amount; let's use $60,000 a year as an example. Some weeks they may work 35 hours and some weeks they may work 50 hours. Regardless of their hours, you still pay them $60,000. A majority of the time, salaried employees are managers or personnel that work on projects. For the most part, these employees receive additional vacation time, sick leave, and periodic bonuses. Salaried staff members are usually the ones who assume most of the responsibilities when operating your business. For example, if you run a call center business, the manager is normally salaried, while the other employees are hourly.

Before you hire a salaried employee, you must identify their job duties by outlining a job description incorporating the various projects, and other requirements up front. This ensures that the employee knows fully what is expected of them.

 *Note: When hiring employees who bring a great deal of knowledge, experience, and dedication to the workplace it is suggested, you offer salary along with added benefits like longer vacation time, bonuses for reaching certain goals, their own office, and so forth. If an employee handles significant amounts of the workload and frees you up to focus on the next step for your business; that employee is deserving of the added benefits. The choice is up to you.*

Paying Employees by Commission

This is a commonly used compensation option, providing your business model possess the means to hire employees and pay them commissions, while retaining profitability. It can prove especially beneficial to business owners, as you can hire several employees at the same time without exceeding your payroll budget. You only pay your employees based on a portion or percentage of the sales they close. You do not have to commit to paying them a salary or hourly wage and can utilize those uncommitted funds elsewhere.

Inside or Outside Sales Reps

Offering commissions to inside or outside sales personnel is a common practice by several companies. Please keep in mind that commissions do not work for all employees or business models. If you hire all sales reps, you must be able to operate the other business functions yourself.

Inside sales mean customers visit your place of business and the sales person guides them through the entire buying process explaining your products (or services), its features, how they function and pricing. An example would be the sales person at a furniture store or car dealership.

Outside sales mean your sales reps will travel away from your company location and visit your customers and/or clients at their place of business, an arranged meeting area, or their home. An outside sales person explains your products (or services), its features, how they function and pricing.

Employees who work on commission should be your sales staff.

For example, employees at the following types of companies are great fits for commission.

- Auto Dealership

- Clothing Store

- Cell Phone Booth or Store

- Advertisement Sales

- Energy or Telecommunication Sales

- Software Sales

> *"Employees who work on commission should be your sales staff."*

Any position involving sales ordinarily work well on commission as long as it remains profitable for your business.

For inside sales reps, you will want to set up a rotation as a result; all commissioned sales reps get a chance to interact with customers.

For outside sales reps, you will want to set location boundaries so the reps are not visiting the same clients.

Having sales reps visit the same business and fight for the commission will definitely not have an agreeable outcome. I have experienced multiple sales reps from the same company try to win my business and it gets ugly.

For both inside and outside sales reps, make sure you have a set of rules for them to follow about fairness and customer interaction.

Commissions are not for all job types

Some business owners offer commissioned jobs to employees who are not actual sales personnel. As sales progress, they soon realize that their commissions are far more than their hourly pay out would have been. Which resulted in loss of profits.

For instance, let's say you own a tutoring service or a music school and offer to pay the teacher 40% of student enrollments instead of the usual $30 per hour.

The teacher is not promoting sales for the school, instead teaching only six hours per session. Let's say one session costs $60 for each student, and 20 students enroll.

$60 (enrollment cost) X 20 (students) = **$1,200**

40% of $1,200 is **$480**, which you pay the teacher.

If you chose the hourly rate of $30 per hour for six hours, you would pay the teacher **$180.**

If you do acquire a partner, make sure you cover every single detail in your contract or agreement.

Let's keep the same scenario but say by the next month 40 students enroll.

$60 (enrollment cost) X 40 (students) = **$2400**

40% of $2,400 is **$960**, which you pay the teacher.

If you chose the hourly rate of $30 per hour for six hours, you would still pay the teacher **$180.**

As you can see as sales progress, keeping a non-sales employee on commission is not a profitable option.

If your business has products or services that sell themselves, and you are conveniently accessible to your customers, inside sales reps are still needed. Only now, it is beneficial to pay them an hourly rate instead of commission. A number of retail stores have stopped paying commissions to their employees since they noticed their products sell without the added push from inside sales reps. Employees now work as a customer service representative instead of a sales rep.

Thus, instead of expending a percentage at every sale you can pay an hourly rate to your employees.

 *Note:* *Before you choose commissions as your preferred method of paying employees, make sure it fits your business model; not doing so could result in lost profits.*

Outsourcing

Outsourcing business tasks means contracting an individual or business staffed to handle your necessary business functions and paying them on a billed or invoice basis instead of hiring an employee.

When outsourcing you do not manage the tasks yourself, instead you assign the task with an agreed upon time for completion and cost.

Outsourcing is commonly performed outside your business although some tasks require an on-location assignment.

An example of outsourcing is hiring an accounting firm to manage the accounting functions of a business, including profit and loss statements, and quarterly and/or yearly tax reporting: instead of doing it yourself or increasing your staff by hiring an accountant. An accounting firm could cost you $300-$400 a month while an employee could cost up to $2,000 a month.

Another example is hiring an answering service to take your calls and direct phone requests from your customers in contrast to hiring three to four employees to take calls.

 Before outsourcing make sure to draw up contracts or agreements with the assigned tasks described in detail with both parties signatures.

Interns

Hiring interns can be a great low cost option for your business as they work for a lower than normal salary or occasionally free. Their goal is work experience within their field of study, and need intern work for credit hours to graduate.

Typically, interns are from educational organizations and work for a specified time. Once their time is up, and they have gained work experience you can hire them as an employee or they move on to other opportunities.

Educational organizations usually require business to have an EIN (which was explained in a previous chapter), have an office or retail space, and a specific job description and position within your company available for interns.

Once these requirements are met, you can contact your local education organizations (colleges, high schools, technical schools, and training schools) to see if they have interns that fit your specific job description and available position. You may also visit your local community center and ask if you can post an ad for interns on their community wall.

Volunteers

Volunteers usually work if your business is focused on helping the community and/or some type of humanitarian cause.

Examples would be a clothing store that gives away a portion of their inventory to families that are going through financial hardships. You can usually turn to social media, your local church or community center to post volunteer opportunities.

Employee Laws & Taxes

Employee Laws

There are many laws concerning employees, and they vary from federal, state, to local laws. Laws differ depending on the industry type, as a result, instead of going over endless information, I will direct you to the Department of Labor website, www.dol.gov, your resource to research, read, and print labor laws for your specific business. You may also use an Internet search engine for "labor laws _____" (enter your state). There you will be guided to the employment laws for your state. Just make sure it includes federal, state, and local laws.

 *Note: You will be required to post different notices in your workspace area for employees. Normally you are able to print them for free from government websites, including a non-discrimination notice, and a minimum wage notice.*

The aforementioned website or Internet search will assist you in making sure you have all the required notices. Besides printing them free there are companies that conveniently offer to put all of your needed notices on a nice laminated poster for a fee. You can find them by doing an Internet search for "labor law posters _____" (enter your state).

Employee Taxes

Listed are required taxes you can expect concerning payroll.

- **Federal Income Tax** – A tax levied by the United States Internal Revenue Service (IRS) on the annual earnings of individuals, corporations, trusts and other legal entities. (Investopedia)

  Good olé Uncle Sam (this one should be self-explanatory). The employees' tax rate is decided based on their deductions and payroll amount. If you are using a payroll service, you do not have to calculate anything. If you are using QuickBooks Payroll or any other payroll software, it should calculate the tax for you. If you wish to calculate it on your own do an Internet search for "federal income tax rates for employee's _____" (enter the tax year).

- **Social Security Tax** – The tax levied on both employers and employees used to fund the Social Security program. Social Security tax is usually collected in the form of payroll tax or self-employment tax. (Investopedia)

  This tax is a fixed rate of 6.2% paid by the employee and 6.2% paid by the employer. This has a maximum dollar limit that seems to vary year by year.

- **Medicare Tax** – the Medicare tax is used to fund the government's Medicare program, which provides subsidized healthcare and hospital insurance benefits to retirees and the disabled. Medicare and Social Security taxes are levied on both employees and employers. (Investopedia.com)

  This tax is also a fixed rate of 1.45% paid by the employee and 1.45% paid by the employer. As of 2013, Medicare taxes have increased by 0.9% to 3.8% for higher-income individuals.

- **Federal Unemployment Insurance** – A source of income for workers who have lost their jobs through no fault of their own. Workers who quit or are fired are generally not eligible for unemployment insurance. Individuals who are self-employed are also not eligible to receive unemployment insurance. (Investopedia.com)

  You will need to register with your nearest unemployment tax office if you are going to process payroll yourself. Do an Internet search for "unemployment insurance _____" (list your state). If you are using a payroll company, they should handle registering for you.

- **State Tax** – Tax levied on income at the state level.

  Rates vary and not all states participate. You will need to inquire with your nearest tax office. Do an Internet search for "State Tax _____" (list your state).

For insurance, 401K, Pension, etc. the organization you use to provide these services for your employees will guide you through the process and deductions.

Payroll Processing Options

- Hire a payroll processing company.
- Use an accounting software that allows you to calculate payroll.

I definitely recommend hiring a payroll company to handle your payroll needs. Generally, you pay a reasonable fee depending on the number of employees. This allows you to focus on operating your business instead of tax rates, filings, paperwork, quarterly tax deposits, check writing, direct deposits, and so on. When you hire a payroll service, usually you are able to email your employee names with hours, and they do the rest. After five years in business, I finally hired a payroll service, and it took a significant amount of stress from me.

Alternatively, do an online search for "payroll software" and explore your options. I use Quickbooks payroll, which worked well until I hired a payroll service.

Employee Policies

Employee Policies (Follow up from Chapter 12 titled, "Business Hours, Company Policies & Agreements")

I touched on the employee policy in another chapter as it tied into company policies. Take note of the additional points to consider plus some repeat advice.

When operating a business with employees, it is extremely important to have a posted policy notice and issue your employees an "Employee Policy Handbook." You can find generic employee policies you can edit to fit your business at your local business supply store in the form of a CD. Alternatively, you can do an Internet search for "Employee Policy Handbook."

Before editing the policies to fit your business, you will need to determine a few things:

1. What are your normal business operating hours?

2. Will employees be paid on a weekly or bi-weekly basis?

3. Will you give bonuses? If so, what will the criteria be to earn a bonus?

4. Are you going to offer vacation time? If so, how long and how long does an employee have to be employed to earn vacation time?

5. Will you give sick pay and for how long?

6. What are the consequences if an employee does not perform their job duties? What if they do not show up for work or come in late repeatedly? Do they receive a verbal warning or are they written up? How many times will you allow it before you have to terminate their employment (fire them)?

Are you going to share with your employees critical business know-how information?

Example – Your business strategies, secret recipes, or factors that pertain to your business that is not general public knowledge, etc.

If so, I suggest you have them sign a non-compete agreement. This form states that if the employee is laid off, fired, or quits they will not start the same type of business and become your competition. A non-compete agreement is enforced customarily for five years after the employee stops working for you.

Once you have answered these questions and set other rules for your employees include them in the Employee Handbook, print, and give it to your employees.

Background Checks, DVR Camera System, Audits

Are your employees going to be handling cash, sensitive documents or anything deemed extremely important to your business? If so, it would be in your best interest to perform an extensive background check on your employee to ensure their history would not compromise the integrity of your business.

If you will have multiple employees, consider having cameras installed with a DVR that records your employees while doing their job. It may seem drastic but if cash and supplies end up missing, or important documents are mishandled, you would have video documentation with the ability to investigate the cause.

There have been many times when having cameras with a DVR system helped remove employees who were not doing what they are supposed to do.

Video surveillance also affords protection for you and your employees as well as your business. Cameras in plain view offer a deterrent for many potential criminals. If there is ever an incident, you will have the video footage needed for an investigation. Subsequently, surveillance is a sound business decision and investment. Be sure to purchase good-quality cameras and a DVR system that assures high-quality results.

Another option to ensure employees are following policy is to have "shoppers" or audits. A shopper meets with you and obtains a list of everything you expect your employee to do, later goes to your business and acts like a normal customer, however, is evaluating your employee on tasks listed.

An auditor is someone who goes into your business and makes sure your employees are following rules, policies, and checks to see if your inventory is accurate.

Final Advice

Never hire employees who come off as rude to leadership, staff, or customers. If you have interacted with employees at any business, perhaps you were subjected to unacceptable customer service a few times yourself. Good employees sometimes may have bad days resulting in unintentionally rude behavior towards customers.

With that in mind you may want to setup policies that will discipline your employees for interacting with a customer rudely or negatively in any way. You never want customers to walk away and think to themselves that they will never do business with you again because of an employee's negative interaction with them.

As a new business owner, you may not be in position to hire or outsource now. This means you will be responsible for every role, responsibility, and task for your company. It can be very challenging but I encourage you to pace yourself and try not to get overwhelmed.

I encourage you to plan a minimum of one day where you do nothing but relax, spend time with those you love, and enjoy the free time. Do not worry, business will always be there waiting for you when you get back.

When it comes to hiring employees one of my golden rules is—

"Do not hire anyone you are not willing to fire."

Chapter 20

Hiring Family & Friends

"You are free to hire whomever you please, just keep in mind my golden rule: Don't hire anyone you are not willing to fire."

Hiring individuals you already know to work for your company has advantages and disadvantages.

Some business owners will tell you that hiring family and friends is a mistake and to keep work and personal life separate. Other business owners will say hiring family and friends brings everyone closer together and is the best decision ever made.

Family

Several family owned businesses operate incredibly effective. Primarily because the family members are professional, understand their position, and work hard to achieve the goals put before them. Hence, it really comes down to attitude, character, and the ability to submit to authority while separating work and beyond workplace relations.

A family member to consider hiring would be someone that is punctual, organized, detail oriented, and motivated.

Make sure to be very clear on your expectations of them and their job duties.

On the other hand, if your relative is constantly let go from jobs, usually late, sleeps on the job, and stays up every night playing video games hiring them might not be the best choice for your business. Those are examples, but you need to determine whether they are eligible for hire based on what you know about them.

I have personally hired and fired family members so you can imagine the awkwardness at family gatherings. I have also experienced hiring family members who went above and beyond their job duties and consequently turned out to be a great decision.

 *Note: If you decide to hire family, I suggest you look at their attitude, current success, and job history. Do not make an emotional decision based on wanting to help your family. Hire and treat them as you would other staff members.*

Friends

Friends are the people you hang out with after work, see movies with, go out to dinner, and so forth. I have always felt it is best to keep friends and business separate because of a few things:

- It can be difficult to separate friendship habits and a professional work environment.

- A friend might think it is OK to do things outside of the normal policies of work because they are your friend and you should not mind or will let things slide.

- If the job does not work out for your friend and you have to let them go, you might be losing an employee as well as a friend.

- Having to discipline your friend during the workday and later go out to dinner might be uncomfortable and awkward.

Another aspect to consider is that your other employees may become upset and feel that you are showing favoritism towards your friend.

Therefore, if you do end up hiring a friend I suggest you set rules and boundaries up front. Have them understand that during work hours you are their boss and treat them the same as you do all employees. I have hired friends and it worked out great because of their professionalism and ability to separate work and personal life. I have fired friends and I can say that every friend I have fired, I have lost.

Developing Friendships with Employees

As an employer you will want to hire people who are not only qualified for the job but also someone you will enjoy working with. During the course of employment, there are chances that you learn about your employees' life outside of work. You may share information about children, interests, values, a common like or dislike for certain types of food, etc. (The list can go on and on).

Over time and during non-work related small talk, some employers develop a bond of friendship with their employees. There can be positive and negative results from this type of friendship. The employee may exhibit more loyalty to the company and work harder but other employees may feel you have "favorites" and believe you treat that employee differently. When it is time to correct a mistake or reprimand that employee, it may or may not put a damper on the friendship, depending on the professional and maturity level of the employee.

> *"When it comes to hiring employees one of my golden rules is "do not hire anyone you are not willing to fire."*

Only you can decide how far you want to bond and develop a friendship with employees. Do it carefully and ensure it does not affect your work environment.

Final Thoughts on Family, Friends, and Developing Friendships

Those closest to me in the workplace are the ones I expect the most from. I am constantly teaching, mentoring, pushing them to excel, and sometimes learning from them. We have developed a strong bond professionally and personally.

Some have moved on because of termination or better opportunities, either way I wish them the best. I make it a habit to tell family or friends before hiring that I will never hold it against them if they find a better opportunity. I have experienced both great pleasure and great pain in hiring family and friends.

You will one day be in a position to hire and will need to decide which option is best for your business. Choose wisely.

> *"A family member to consider hiring would be someone that is punctual, organized, detail oriented, and motivated."*

Allowing Couples (Married or Dating) to Work for You

There are companies that allow married or dating couples within their company and other companies that have strict rules against it. Larger companies sometimes allow it as long as they work in different departments. I have seen it work very well when working in different departments; I have also seen it not work at all when working close together.

When setting up your workplace policies you need to decide if you will allow couples, whether dating or married to work within your company. As a result, I want to make sure you know what could happen if couples work close together.

- Couples working together may be more interested in each other than getting the job done.

- If one employee in the relationship is excessively jealous, there definitely will be consequences if their significant other is flirty or overly friendly to other employees or customers.

- If there is a death or family emergency, you will be asked by both employees for time off.

- The couple will frequently want vacation time together.

- If there are arguments at home, it may well be carried over to the job.

- If you have to discipline, write up, or scold an employee their significant other may want to become involved when it is not their business.

- If you must terminate an employee, their significant other may resent you. They may not perform work at their fullest potential and eventually quit which results in losing two employees instead of one.

Working with Your Spouse

If you are a new business and working with your spouse, you may experience days where it is the best choice you ever made as well as days where you need to step away and take a break. When there is no separation from home life and work life things might become a little frustrating here and there, though that is based on your relationship with each other and not for me to determine.

If you are going to run your business with your spouse, I suggest you both have separate job duties and responsibilities.

I also suggest you set a time where you stop working and focus on each other. If you are working from home you might want to separate a space, dedicated to your business and after working hours, shut the door and be done for the day.

> *"Working with your spouse can be very rewarding (and challenging at times) and a very beautiful thing if you approach it the right way."*

In some cases one spouse may keep a normal day job while the other works on the company. This allows a steady flow of income without having to use the company's income for personal use in the beginning stages. Some business owners have decided to give it all they have and both spouses work in the business together. This option is very risky unless you have a proven business model.

I hope this chapter has given you further insight and will help you have a clearer understanding of what your options are when deciding to hire.

As a new business owner, you may not be in position to hire or outsource now. This means you will be responsible for every role, responsibility, and task for your company. I encourage you to pace yourself and try not to get overwhelmed.

 I encourage you to plan a minimum of one day where you do nothing but relax, spend time with those you love, and enjoy the free time. Do not worry, business will always be there waiting for you when you get back.

Chapter 21

Advertising & Marketing
(Learn How to Reach Your Customers)

"How can customers buy your products or services if they do not know you exist?"

Advertising and marketing are one of the most important aspects of running a successful business. Your goal is to make sales but how can you if no one knows your business exists?

Advertising and marketing will either cost you time and money or both so make sure you fit this into your plans because not doing so could result in having a business with no customers.

And no customers— means no business.

Let's begin.

Advertising and Marketing

Advertising - The process of making your product or service known to the marketplace. This is your business on a printed ad, billboard, commercial, radio announcement, banner, Internet ad, and so forth. Typically, anything containing your business name and brief company information that is displayed can be considered an advertising method.

Marketing - This is the process of preparing your product or service for the marketplace. This process includes concept or original idea, design, packaging, pricing, advertising, selling and delivery. (Investopedia)

Four P's of Marketing - Marketing companies refer to this as the four P's, "The activities of a company associated with buying and selling a product or service. It includes advertising, selling and delivering products to people. People who work in marketing departments of companies try to get the attention of target audiences by using slogans, packaging design, celebrity endorsements and general media exposure. The four 'Ps' of marketing are product, place, price and promotion". (Investopedia)

Hiring an Agency - You could hire an advertising agency to manage your ad purchasing for you. They generally charge for developing your advertisements and receive a percentage of the amount you spend with the advertiser. Make sure you determine your cost directly from the advertiser, then figure your cost using an agency. It may be less expensive, the same, or more expensive to use an agency. Overall, you can decide to use an agency according to cost and the time it will free you up to focus on other aspects of your business. Time is money. Depending on how much the agency works with different advertisers will determine the types of discounts they receive and pass on to you. Some agencies require monthly commitments, so make sure to check their requirements before meeting with them.

To find an advertising agency do an online search for "marketing or advertising companies in _____ (list your city). They will want to know the type of business you are in, your monthly budget, and goals. Make sure you check with a couple of agencies before deciding which one fits best for your industry and company. You will want to view their previous or current success stories and advertisement campaigns.

Doing it Yourself - Several business owners choose to handle their own advertising and marketing campaign for various reasons and are very successful. If you choose this route you will be in charge of determining which advertising methods work best for your business, as well as what your ads should read or say (if a commercial). This chapter will give you some insight on marketing options and how to approach companies you wish to place advertisements with.

You will need to narrow down your target market, set your advertising budget, understand your advertising methods, and learn how to communicate effectively. Also, make sure you factor in time for research and negotiating the price of ads.

Marketing and Advertising Campaign - For a marketing or advertising campaign, you first have to determine some basic information. We will go through every detail in steps; along with questions for you to answer, then go over different advertising and marketing options. As always, it is your responsibility to determine which method is best for your business.

Target Market

*Your "target market" is the consumers who most likely need, want,
and buy your products or services.*

First

Determining Your Target Market - Each question may not pertain to your business. Try your best to answer as thorough as possible. You will use your answers to help you determine which advertising strategies best fit your business.

List the age group most likely to purchase your product or service. Example (18-25 years)

_____

Are your customers usually male, female, or would both genders most likely purchase your products or services?

_____

What educational background would your customers usually have? (Grade school, high school, college, etc.)

_____

What is the average yearly income of the people most likely to purchase from you?

_____

Are your potential customers most likely married or single?

_____

Do your potential customers live in a house, apt, condo, loft, etc.?

_____

What areas do your customers live in? (If multiple cities or areas list them all)

_____

_____

_____

_____

Write any other information about your customers that will help you categorize them.

_____

_____

_____

_____

_____

_____

_____

Your answers should give you a clear picture of where your potential customers are and who to gear your advertising towards.

When you communicate with companies to advertise with they will give you a breakdown of the type of audiences they reach. Your answers should be very similar to that audience.

Second

Know Your Customers

If you are a new business, use your knowledge and experience in your business type to answer these questions. If you are an existing business then you should have a good idea of the answers.

What type of advertisements do they most likely respond to?

_____

_____

_____

_____

What factors do they consider when deciding to purchase and become loyal repeat customers? Quality, price, convenience, location, etc.

_____

_____

_____

_____

_____

Understand your customers' habits by knowing where your customers go, what do they do, and their interests.

Do the majority of your customers go to the mall, shop on the Internet or shop at discount stores?

_____

Where are your customers most likely to see your advertisements? Example: outdoors, TV, Internet, etc.

_____

_____

_____

What type of magazines do they read? Fashion trends, automotive, business, home and garden, sports, etc.?

_____

Do they enjoy sports, indoor or outdoor recreations? What do they do in their spare time?

_____

Do they live in low, middle, or high-income areas?

_____

Do they wear dress slacks/business suits, casual clothing, t-shirt and jeans, or uniforms to work?

_____

When your customers watch TV, what networks do they usually watch?

_____

What industries do your customers work in?

_____

Where do your customers usually go? Church, shopping, night clubs, restaurants, etc.

_____

_____

What do your customers do? Hike, run, bake, swim, watch TV, dance, etc.

_____

_____

List other customer habits in reference to their life style.

_____

_____

You should now have a clear understanding as to where your customers go, what they do, and their interests.

 One of the major goals of a business owner is to place advertisements in areas they are most likely to see them. Using advertisements that tailor to customers' interests will get their attention.

Example: If you sell sports equipment, your ads could have individuals playing sports in your equipment at a football game, baseball game, soccer field, etc. Someone who loves football will be drawn to your ad because of their interest.

Now that you have their attention, give them a reason to buy your product or service.

Third

Determine Your Advertising Budget and Face-To-Face Marketing Time

How much money do you have to invest in an advertising campaign? List the amount on a monthly basis.

_____

You can consider the amount listed to be your advertising budget.

As you operate your business, you will notice some advertisements work better than others. Once you decide which advertising method works best, focus your budget on that method.

Face-to-face marketing is typically carried out by sales people who visit potential customers at their place of business, home, or event, etc.

If your business requires face-to-face marketing, when are you available to market your business? List days and hours.

_____

The time listed is when you need to focus on marketing your products or services.

The answers you provided have helped you determine your target market, where potential customers are most likely to view your advertisements, and your marketing budget.

Once you read and understand the different methods, you will be able to decide which options are best for your business.

 **Tips**

- Appearance and first impressions are extremely important. Make sure you, your staff, and your location is up to par in such a way that your customers will have a positive impression.

- When conversing with any potential customers always determine who the decision maker is and who or what influences them to make a purchase.

- If you have a "repeat" business, then retaining your customers is very important. Reward them with discounts or free items for their loyalty!

- Do what it takes to "wow" your customers. Let your service be so amazing that they tell their friends and family about it. Remember, a happy customer is a "referring" customer.

Access Referrals

Outside of your target market there is another option that I personally call **"Access Referrals".**

Access Referrals targets a group of individuals who are not your target market but have access to them and can refer customers (their family or friends) to you. Have you ever said "I bet my "mom" would really like this?" Or perhaps, instead of your mom maybe another family member or friend. People are constantly communicating their daily life and experiences with each other. And sometimes those experiences include products or services that could cater to someone they know.

"Never underestimate the chance of someone knowing someone who could use your product or service."

Let's say you own a boutique shop called "Bella's Boutique" and it caters to middle school, high school and college-aged girls.

Instead of merely advertising direct to your target market, you could also advertise to their parents who in turn refers their daughter to your boutique or it results in the parent buying something for her. Your ads could read something like this:

"Are you proud of your High School grad? She deserves the best. Give her the gift of Bella's Boutique."

"Hey Dad, looking for the perfect gift for your daughter? No worries, we have gift assist professionals here to help"

"Nothing says mother and daughter bonding better than boutique shopping!"

"World's best Dad badges earned here!"

"No matter how far your daughter travels for college she will always be your little girl. —Free Shipping."

The ads can go on, but I believe you get the point. All you have to do is apply the concept to your own business.

My suggestion is to use this method only if you already have an established business and customer base.

If you are a first time new business owner, I suggest focusing on your target market first, and then try targeting "access referrals" cautiously and in increments if you determine it will be beneficial.

Advertising & Marketing Options

 *Note: It is very important for you to communicate with your customers and find out how they heard about your business. In doing so, you can determine which advertising options worked best; as a result, you can increase that option or explore similar ones.*

Billboards – This option will give your business 24 hour exposure (if the billboard is lit at night) to every vehicle that passes by. However, you only have a few seconds to "speak" to your customers (unless your billboard is at a stop light) so it is best to not have too much information on there. Try to be as brief as possible by giving your customers the major information needed for them to contact your business. I suggest using your business name, slogan, major product or service you offer, then a very easy to remember phone number, website address, or exit now arrow (exit now arrows will only work if your billboard is at the exit of your business).

Let's use a Bar & Grill Restaurant as an example.

When deciding to place a phone number on the ad, it should be very easy to remember.

Example: (777)-222-EATS or (777)222-RIBS.

The website listed on the billboard should be a name people can easily remember like www. GreatSteaks.com. You are able to have more than one website name that will lead to your actual website.

Example:

If your business name is Texas Ranch Restaurant, LLC then you could have a website domain name called www.TexasRanchRestaurant.com and you can also have www. GreatSteaks.com or www.iHeartSteaks.com, etc. and point them all to your main website www.TexasRanchRestaurant.com.

If you are unsure as to how to do this, contact the person or company that developed your website and they should be able to guide you through the process or do it for you.

If you are interested in leasing a billboard, here are a couple of options.

Option 1- Drive around and find billboards that state they are available for lease. Generally, billboards have a phone number you can call for pricing information. If not, they frequently have the company name somewhere small on the billboard, and you can find them by doing an Internet search.

Option 2- You can do an Internet search for "billboards in _____ (list your city)" and several options will be listed for which you can choose.

When speaking with the sales representative about leasing a billboard remember that the sales rep is going to try to get the highest monthly payment for the billboard so you may have to do some serious negotiation (Negotiating will be covered under Chapter 23 titled, "Sales & Negotiating"). The longer you lease the billboard the greater are your chances of lowering the monthly rate.

Billboard companies normally have graphic artists that can help design your ad. Make certain you forward them your logo and business colors in order to keep a branded look for your company. Each billboard company is different as far as terms but you could expect to sign a 3, 6, 12 months or more.

A similar yet less expensive option is to ask the billboard company if they offer posters. Posters are a much smaller version of billboards and cost less. Finally, digital billboards are another option if available in your area; you will be sharing advertising space with a rotating digital ad and sharing the cost as well. Your billboard representative will be able to give you a full list of options, prices, and terms.

Paper (Print) Ads – Companies throughout the US have established themselves by delivering newspapers, classified ads, and so forth to readers. They make their money from advertisers. Depending on which city you live in determines which paper ads are available. Generally, there are papers that are tailored to the buyer looking for a deal, individuals looking to keep up with the news, papers catering to the young adult party nightlife and several others depending on your city.

Take a tour of the areas your customers' most likely work, live or visit and pick up the local papers in the area. Grocery stores, corner stores, restaurants, and bus stops, are normally filled with paper ads for you to pick up.

Once you have several papers, look through them and ask yourself, which one (or more) are your customers likely to read? It may be one or a number of the papers.

Next, look at the different ads currently in the paper. This gives you a general idea of the sections the paper provides along with your sizing options. Most papers are divided into sections per advertising specialty, and some papers will allow you to place your ad anywhere.

Write down which ads caught your attention and gave you the most valuable information.

It is obvious that larger ads draw your attention quicker; however, they substantially cost more than mid to smaller size ads. Look at the smaller ads that caught your attention and see how they are different from the other small ads that you noticed afterwards.

If you decide this form of advertising is for you. The publisher's information along with a phone number to call for advertising can be found somewhere within the paper. Call them for additional information. Your business type, the size of the ad, and how long you want to run the ad is necessary to acquire an accurate quote.

 It is recommended that you ask for a "media kit." Media kits are commonly emailed and contain important information. For example, how long they have been in business, how many papers are distributed to homes or in stores, which areas they are distributed to, how frequent the papers are distributed (daily, weekly, monthly), and the breakdown of their readers by income, age, nationality, and so on. Many media kits come with pricing that can be negotiated.

Most sales reps will ask you to commit to an average of six to eight weeks to test the success of the ad for your business. These reps are trained to ask for longer commitments and obtain a signed agreement from you. If you are asked to sign an agreement for longer than six distribution periods, you can tell them you want to make sure the ad works before agreeing to anything long term. In some cases, you may also choose to advertise weekly with no contracts.

It may take some going back and forth with the sales rep because their job is to sell ads and get your commitment. Your job is to make sure this advertising method is cost-effective and profitable for your business.

Business Cards - Every business should have their own set of business cards. They should be given out every time contact is made with a potential customer. The information on them should be precise and direct. An example could be your business name, logo, your name, title, contact information, and slogan on one side and your primary products or services on the other side.

Depending on your type of business you can hire someone (or do it yourself) to pass out business cards to prospective customers.

Post Cards - Think of a post card as a larger business card that has additional information. With post cards, you can list your business name, logo, slogan, location, and contact information on one side while you have products and services on the other side. Alternatively, you could make one side in English and one side in another language in case your customer base may speak multiple languages. Keep in mind that you do not want to overdo it with a lot of cluttered info, so stick with the most important aspects of your business. Post cards can be passed out hand to hand and direct mailed to potential customers.

Brochures - Brochures are a professionally visual method to share a detailed explanation of your business and offerings. Brochures are usually given out to your potential customers at your place of business and you could ask other businesses that cater to your target market to place them on their brochure racks if available. You can also rent a booth at a community event and pass them out or you can mail them directly to your target market.

> *"As you operate your business, you will notice some advertisements work better than others."*

Flyers - This option is an especially cost effective way to get the details of your business known by several potential customers.

Flyers are typically distributed door to door or in a market place where your customers frequent. Flyers can be placed on community boards or windows of existing businesses (with permission). Flyers are designed in various sizes, can be printed front and back in color or black & white. You can choose to have one side in English and the other side in another language or choose to use the backside for additional business information.

Mail Outs – This method comes with several different options.

Every single day in the United States, our postal workers are hard at work delivering mail to every house, apartment, and business.

Unfortunately, much of that mail is commonly labeled "junk mail" and if you are the person at home or place of business that opens the daily mail, you know exactly what I am writing about. However, if you find an option that works for you, it is a great way to advertise directly to existing or potential customers. The only way to know for sure is to try it and see what works.

No matter which option you choose you will need to create a "mail out" piece. Think of what types of mail get your attention and what leads to you opening or looking at it is a good start to figure out the concept for your mail piece.

Option 1 – With today's technology and never-ending requests for surveys, data mining (collection) companies have captured information on numerous people or households and categorized it into databases. These databases contain lists of addresses, emails, phone numbers, and interests. They are divided into categories, and supplied to businesses for purposes of marketing directly to them.

Lists can range from several hundred to several thousand contacts. To find these companies simply do an Internet search for "mailing list", "direct-mail marketing, or mail marketing." You will find several companies that provide this service for you. I would suggest that you look into several companies and compare accuracy, pricing, and guarantees before deciding which company to use. While shopping around keep in mind that some companies just provide a list while others will do all of the work for you, which includes printing your advertising piece, applying postage, and mailing your piece for you.

"Your goal is to get your business information in front of your potential customers."

Option 2 – You can do a mass mail out by zip code or an area within a zip code. Let's say you own a business that caters to a specific area of town. By using this option, you will be able to let all of the residents and local businesses know that you are now able to offer them your products or services. To utilize the service go to www.USPS.com, click on <u>Business Solutions</u>, then <u>Advertise with Mail</u>. Next, you will read the options, which are generally found under "Customized Market Mail" or "Every Door Direct Mail." There are phone numbers for you to call for additional info. You will find samples on the website giving you a visual example of what they do for your business mail piece.

Option 3 – There are companies that focus on combining businesses wishing to advertise through mail outs in the same area, and everyone shares the cost. If you are the person who opens and distributes the mail, you have possibly received packets of coupons, post cards, and local advertiser information, bundled in plastic wrapping or in a large envelope. This is commonly called "shared mail advertising" and can be very cost-effective as well as beneficial, if you are able to produce an advertising piece that stands out above the rest.

 On one hand, you are sharing the mail-out cost with other businesses saving you lots of money but on the other hand, you have to compete with the same businesses for potential customers' attention.

Do an Internet search for "shared mail advertising " to find companies that offer this service.

Email Service

Just like mail-out lists, there are email lists as well. People have given their email addresses and given permission to receive promotional emails from businesses that are in the category of their interests.

Sending mass emails allow your businesses products and services to be seen by a large group of potential customers. Your goal is get them to open it and your email to not end up in their spam folder.

Ask yourself what causes you to open emails, ignore or trash them? Some businesses will use catchy subject lines or simply offer their products or services as the subject.

If you wish to use an email service simply, do an Internet search for "email list." You will find many companies to choose from that sell you a list of email addresses of potential customers who at one point agreed to receive emails based on their interests in a specific category. Make certain you ask them if they have any type of guarantee that your email will not end up in a spam folder.

 *Note: Your email should include an option to "unsubscribe" from receiving any future emails.*

When interacting with your customers be sure to ask if they wish to subscribe to your email list. You will be able to promote specials, sales, etc. directly to them.

Social Media –Facebook, Twitter, Instagram, YouTube, etc.

This method of advertising is unique in the fact that you can advertise your business to thousands of people for little to no cost.

Let's go over some social media outlets and discuss how they work.

Facebook – If you have a Facebook account you should be familiar with how it can work for business but for those of you who do not, I will explain it for you.

Facebook allows users to connect with hundreds to several thousands of other users by "Liking" their business page.

For businesses, you would create a "business page," and ask your customers to "Like" your page. The "friends" of your customers will see your business page on their "news feed," and they have the opportunity to decide if your products or services are something they would want to purchase or "Like" as well.

With your business page, you will be able to upload pictures, write specials, and communicate with your customers directly (as long as they "Like" your page).

If you are interested in creating a Facebook page visit www.Facebook.com and create an account then select "Create a Page." Follow the directions from there.

Facebook also has a sponsored ad program, which allows your posts to be visible to users who may have interest in your products or services. For more information, visit Facebook. com/ads.

Twitter works a little differently, as users have followers. You would create an account and have your current customers "follow you." By doing that, you are able to promote your business, write messages your customers will read as well as post pictures. To set up a Twitter account, visit their home page at Twitter.com. It is a simple process and self-explanatory.

Instagram works by users having followers as well. However, instead of sending your customers messages you would promote your business through pictures.

Ask your current customers to "follow you" and every time you upload a picture, your customers may see it. They also have an option to "like it." When a "follower" of your customer looks at your customer's page, they have an option to see the photos your customer has liked. They can then follow, like, and determine if they have interest in your products or services. Along with pictures, you are able to upload text on a picture, thus, your customers are able to read your message as well.

To setup an Instagram account visit Instagram.com and follow the steps.

Youtube.com works by users or businesses uploading videos to their channel and putting it into a category and utilizing tag words. Your customers will need to know your youtube.com profile name to view the videos that you post and share it with others. To set up a Youtube.com account simply visit YouTube.com, select "Sign in", then create an account. From there you will just follow the steps.

Although only four social media sites were used as an example there are countless others and new sites being created frequently.

I suggest you use social media sites to promote your business.

Which social media sites should you choose?

Determine which sites your potential customers are most likely to use then register accounts with them.

Make Sure To...

Have social media icons on your website, brochures, and any other advertisement you send out to attract more customers. You can offer coupons or discounts on your social media sites so your customers are drawn to your social media pages. Remember, every time you post a message, picture or video the better chances you have for potential customers to see your business products or services.

What if I am unfamiliar with social media in general?

For a better understanding on how each of these social media methods work; I encourage you to visit their website pages, look up videos on YouTube.com that explain how they work, or simply ask a teenager.

Final Advice for Social Media

Make sure while using social media to promote your products or services you also use it to simply to say, "thank you" to your customers. You can use it to send out encouraging messages or promote your favorite holidays and so forth.

"If people see your business has a personality, their experience with your business may be more favorable and not just about money exchanging hands."

Text Message Service

These days a majority of people are text messaging each other instead of calling. There is a service that allows you to collect your customers or potential customers phone numbers and send periodic text message updates on your business, specials or promotions. There is typically a character count limit. Meaning you are limited to the amount of text you can send.

Most services will assign your business a keyword and your customers will simply text "your keyword" to the short code assigned, and they will start receiving text messages from you immediately.

To find businesses that offer this service do an Internet search for "text message service", make sure to compare rates and text messaging limits.

TV Commercials

Running commercials allow you to reach your specific audience according to the networks your customers watch and the area where they live.

You can start in the right direction to air your commercial by calling your local cable company. You need to ask for a "media kit" which provides all the networks available that fit your business industry, the areas where their commercials run and a breakdown of how many cable subscribers are in each area.

Cable companies can offer an "Entire City Package" which means whatever network you choose your commercial will air throughout the entire city. On the other hand, you can choose which areas in your city for your commercial to air. Your job is to determine with the help of your sales person at the cable company, which networks your customers, are most likely to watch and areas where they live.

Develop a commercial that grabs your customer's attention and easily allows viewers to understand what products or services you offer. An easy to remember phone number or website should be on display the entire time. The cable company should be able to help produce a commercial or refer you someone who can.

You need to estimate a budget for producing the commercial and a plan for your airtime. Airtime is considered every time your commercial airs on the networks. The cost may be more affordable than you think. Then again, that depends on the city, networks, and frequency your commercial runs. The only way to know for sure is to contact your local cable provider for a media kit.

Radio Commercials

Radio advertising can be challenging, considering your listeners do not have anything to write down your information as most of them are driving. You only have a few seconds to catch your listeners' attention so make sure to use them wisely.

Determine which radio station your customers are most likely to listen to and contact them for a media kit. Keep in mind that some listeners, including me, ignore radio commercials and just switch to another station unless the first commercial grabs my attention. Make sure your commercial includes an easy to remember website, location, or phone number.

 Aside from your local radio stations keep in mind that there are numerous online radio stations, XM radio, or even apps that provide music to their listeners (Pandora for example).

Marketing Face-to-Face (usually for non-retail businesses)

There is nothing like meeting your prospective clients in person so they know firsthand about the products and services your business offers. Now keep in mind there are other competing businesses doing the same thing by visiting your potential customers in order to gain their business. You can approach marketing your business by simply showing up at the doorstep of your prospective clients, send an introductory email, give them a phone call to set up an appointment, or reach them by mail, hoping they contact you. You need to determine which way is the best option for your business.

The saying "never judge a book by its cover" does not apply to face-to-face marketing. You will be judged by your appearance, voice tone, approach, product knowledge and overall professionalism.

Here are a few things to keep in mind when marketing.

- Always dress professional.

- Keep plenty of business cards, brochures, and any other marketing materials on hand.

- Be ready to give your potential clients prices, dates of service/delivery, and discounts.

- Be prepared to be told you are not welcome and turned away. This could happen if you do not have a set appointment time or if the business you are visiting is not in need of your products or services.

- When you do meet in person with the decision maker, make sure you know the lowest possible dollar amount you are able to offer for your products or services.

- Be ready to explain in detail your products and services.

- Be ready to explain why they should use your business instead of your competition.

- Every agreement should be in writing.

- IMPORTANT- Do not make the mistake of only talking about your products and services while giving the impression you only care about making a sale. Make some time for small talk and get to know your potential client. Find out personal things about them like where they grew up or if they like dogs, fishing, etc. Find a common interest and talk about it. People prefer to do business with other people they like and enjoy talking to. Many deals are made because a sales person is relating rather than pushing.

It may take several companies turning you down before you make a sale. Never give up, review your strategy, and make changes in your approach if necessary.

Cold Calling

This option may be more challenging as you are calling a client (whether business or individual) when they are not expecting your call. You may be confronted with the response that the person you are looking for is not available; you may get a hang up, transferred to voice-mail, or you may actually get to talk to the right person. Now if you are calling an individual keep in mind that dinnertime and weekends are more than likely not the best times to be making that call. If you are calling a medium to large business, you will almost certainly never speak to the owner. Instead, you may speak to the employee who manages that department and decides whether to use your product or service.

If you are calling a small business, normally the owner or secretary will be the one answering the phone. You literally have a few seconds to either catch their attention or be completely disregarded.

A Few Suggestions When Cold Calling

Do not be overly direct when cold calling.
How many times have you picked up the telephone and heard this on the other end?

Hello, My name is _____ from "Any Business", and I was wondering if you have a few minutes so I can go over my products or services?

What was your response? Did your guard come up? Did you write them off as a soliciting phone call? Was your sole intention after that point to get them off the phone?

The answer is most likely "yes" and if your answer is "no" you are probably one of the most patient people in the world.

Most people usually do not have a few minutes to listen to you talk about your products or services.

Being more aware of your potential clients time can lead to them lowering their guard and giving you the opportunity to listen to what you have to say.

The call could be more like this, "Hello, my name is _____ from "My Business"; I would like to mail or email you some information about my products/services (choose which one, products or services). Can you verify your mailing address or would an email be better?

They may respond with "What product/service is it?" You can then go into further details. At least at this point, you have their attention. Once they hear you out they may give you a mailing or email address, or tell you they do not need your products or services.

Be sure to give a follow-up call in the next couple of days to inquire if they received your business information by mail or email.

There are other cold calling scripts for you to research and receive advice.

Research other cold calling tips and try different methods until you determine what works best for you.

Referrals

 This is without a doubt the best form of advertising.

Referrals work out great because they do not cost you anything and you have creditability on your products or services from the start.

Have you ever eaten at a great restaurant where the food was absolutely delicious and the service was excellent? Have you ever experienced the best customer service while purchasing a product? If so, you possibly told other people about your experiences. This is not directly intentional but similar to what many refer to as second nature.

"Customer satisfaction is priceless."

Its benefits will follow you in the form of repeat business and referrals.

Your customers have friends, family, co-workers, etc. They will encounter people that your advertising strategies may never reach.

These people may be in need of your products or services and who can better refer them than your very satisfied customers.

Potential customers are most likely to purchase from your business if they have a referral instead of trying out a business they know nothing about.

Getting your customers to refer your business is as simple as asking them to do so.

Ask your customer - Are you satisfied with our service or product? If your customer answers yes, ask them to refer others that need your product or service. Ask them to "Like" or "Follow" your business on their social media accounts.

"Customer satisfaction is priceless."

If the answer is no, then ask what you can do to fix the problem.

Do as much as you can (within reason) to get your customers to say "yes" to your question before the end of the business transaction which will ensure you getting positive feedback.

 **Note:** *Realistically there is no way to please every single customer every time. No matter how much you try, it just will never happen.*

Remember, just as easy as it is for your customers to refer your business, they can also tell others how horrible their experience was.

Promote Directly to Potential Customers (Face-to-Face Marketing)

Have you ever been to an event (sports, indoor car show, fashion, etc.) and seen people handing out sample or promotion products to those who pass by? If so, you witnessed a form of promoting directly to potential customers.

Promoting directly guarantees a 100% potential customer exposure. You will need to do some research and decide where a majority of potential customers are going to be. Then you (or a hired team) will hand out samples of your product, a promotional product or an advertisement of services right into their hands.

 Promotional products along with product samples or advertising materials can be given out free, especially when you go to events, stores, apartment complexes, home building offices, office buildings, grocery stores, parking lots, business conferences, and all that is similar. Practically, any place your potential customers gather is a good place to promote directly to them.

Promotional items can be anything from pens, markers, balloons, small footballs, key chains, baseballs, magnets, calendars, cups, and so on. The basic idea is to connect directly with your customers by handing out fun or useful items with your company name, logo, and contact information (phone number, website, etc.) to the general public and more importantly to your potential customers.

Whether you are handing out product samples, promotional items, or advertising materials it is most effective on a large scale, where you can hand them out to several hundred people at one time.

Picture this: you own a bakery and want to do Guerrilla Marketing. You do research and find out where and when there is a gathering of potential customers (or you could stand right outside your bakery). You make several sample batches of your best product and give them out for free along with information they need to continually purchase more from you.

In order to make this type of marketing successful you need to make sure the people or businesses you are marketing to are potential customers or clients. Doing your research beforehand is crucial.

If you are giving away sample products (not promotional items), make sure it is an item or items customers are able to buy repeatedly. Otherwise, you will end up giving away your profits. Back to the bakery concept, if people love your baked goods they are most likely to become repeat customers.

As with all forms of marketing make sure you do a test run to determine how effective your marketing plan is working. Not doing so will quickly deplete your budget.

Internet Ads & Search Engines

There are so many options within this advertising method it is not feasible to discuss all of them. However, I will go over the most popular and common ways to advertise your business on the Internet.

If you have visited popular websites like Yahoo.com, Facebook.com, Google.com, and others, you should be familiar with ads at the top of the page and on the sides. Your goal is to place your ad on websites where potential customers are likely to visit.

Search engine websites (example: Google, Yahoo) usually allow businesses to register with them at no cost. They also offer "pay per click" advertising, which allows your ad to display in search results and you pay a certain amount every time someone clicks your ad.

Other non-search engine websites usually allow a monthly payment for your ad to be listed on their site with no click limit.

Search Engines

There are so many search engines out there but some of the popular ones are Google. com, Yahoo.com, Bing.com, Yelp.com and YellowPages.com. I might be missing some, but you get the basic idea. Register with as many search engines as you possibly can and only pay-per-click advertise on the search engines that your potential customers are likely to use. By doing so increases your chances of your business being viewed by users who are in your target market.

When registering your business on any search engine be sure to use keywords that most users will normally type when searching for businesses that offer your products or services. In this way, your business may pull up in organic (non-paid) search results.

Once you figure out which search engines you want to use "pay-per-click" advertising with, you need to contact their advertising or sales department and get an overview of how their advertisement works, their costs, and conditions.

For example, if you own an automotive repair company a user can visit Google.com and type in the search engine bar "auto repair in Austin" and a list of auto repair companies in Austin will show in the results. The difference is that your ad will either show up on the very top, on the side, or the bottom of one of the results pages and will be highlighted as a "Sponsored Ad." Keep in mind that since other companies are able to pay for sponsored ads you will be competing with them to see which sponsored ads appear and in what order.

You will be able to set up a specific daily budget to ensure that you will not go over what you have agreed to spend on pay per click advertising. To set up "pay per click" you need to obtain a list of your industry's key words. Key words are specific words that users may use to search for your industry, products or services. Let's use an auto shop for an example; key words could be "auto repair shop", "oil change," "muffler repair," "engine work" and so on.

Specific Websites

Some sites allow you to pay advertising fees on a monthly basis, which cover an unlimited amount of clicks without paying extra. These websites are usually focused toward a specific audience. Many of these sites cover a variety of different categories for your ad placement.

These sites may offer advertising packages divided by area, city, or state. "Area" is having your ad shown when people from a specific side of town visit the site. An example would be an auto repair company on the North side of town, and the majority of their customers are from the North side as well. Therefore, the specific website should be able to place your ad in front of potential customers who are visiting the site from an area that is in the North side of town.

You will not need key words for this option, as the site will place your ad by either your industry category, home page, subcategory page or on a search engine within the website. (If placed on a search engine within the website you may need to use key words depending on the website's policies).

For more detailed information, visit websites your potential customers are likely to look up and ask them for advertising details. If they allow advertisers, they will be able to guide you through the entire process.

Magazines

If you have ever picked up a magazine, you already know that they are full of advertisements.

 Nearly all magazines are tailored to a specific audience. Consequently, if you wanted to advertise in one, you need to determine which magazine your customers are most likely to read.

You can find a variety of magazines at grocery stores, bookstores, some pharmacies and retail stores like Walmart. You may purchase or browse through the magazines your potential customers are most likely to read and find the publisher's contact information. If their contact information is not listed, you can find it by doing an Internet search. Once you contact the magazine, ask about what type of advertising options they provide and request a media kit.

Some magazines may only allow well-known branded national, international, or global companies advertise, while some magazines allow small businesses to advertise. It depends solely on the magazines' guidelines.

Cost depends on the size of the ad, frequency (how long you want your ad to run), and whether you are going to run city, state, or nationwide. Some magazines will offer a city-by-city breakdown so you can target your customers specifically, while other magazines have nationwide distribution options. Because there are so many magazine choices, you need to consult with them directly to see what options would be the best fit for your business and your budget.

Something to keep in mind.

When researching magazines that your potential customers are likely to read you may come across a few not so known magazines that have not been around too long. Before advertising with them first ask how many subscribers they have, how did they get those subscribers, how much are subscriptions, where are their distribution points, and verify how long they have been in business. You can also ask for a new advertiser discount.

Lastly, never pay in advance for multiple months unless you know for certain the magazine ad (or any ad) produces results for your business.

Door-To-Door

Door to door advertising is exactly what the name says. A person or a group of people will go house to house (or business to business) in a specific area and leave an advertising piece either on or by their front door. They may also knock on the door and talk to the homeowners about business products or services.

Business cards, post cards, door hangers, or flyers are the most common types of printed advertising pieces businesses choose to use when door to door advertising. Door hangers are an advertising piece where the top has been cut to make a hook shape, which fits over most doorknobs.

If you choose this method you need to either do the work yourself, hire someone or a group of people, or you may hire a business that sends out a team on a regular basis.

Providing you decide to hire a business, do an online search for "door to door advertising in _____ (list your city), go through the list of advertisers by calling and requesting their rates and service offerings. The company normally requires payment upfront and will need the advertising materials, and a map of where you want them to deliver your ads. The only way to know absolutely if your advertisements are delivered is to check on the area during their route delivery.

224

Unfortunately, there are many cases where individuals distributed less than half of the materials they were given. The remaining handouts were trashed and the individuals go on break until their time is up. This has happened to many businesses, so do not let it happen to you.

 *Note: If you choose to use door to door as an advertising method be careful to not leave anything on or in a mailbox. Mailboxes are federal property and you could get penalized for doing so.*

City or Community Events (Booth Rental)

Depending on where your business is located, there should be some type of organized event where groups of people gather for fun, entertainment, and shopping. Usually your city or community will host a function together and offer booth rentals to local businesses (Example: car show, boat show, garden show, fashion expos, community fun days, etc.). *If you feel like the event will cater to your potential customers, it would be a great opportunity for you to rent a booth and communicate directly to your target market.*

If you need help finding out when these events take place, call your neighborhood community center, local schools and colleges, sporting arenas, major shopping complexes, convention centers, or your cities' government office that caters to tourism.

Another way to find events in your city is to do an online search for "events in _____ (list your city). Choose the events that cater to businesses or individuals that could be your potential customers.

Once you have determined which events, call and inquire about renting a booth. Make sure to ask for the different booth sizes and which ones are expected to have the most foot traffic. If you require electricity be sure to ask for that as well and get a clear understanding of their rules and guidelines for the event.

 *Note: Make your booth attractive enough to draw people's attention. Make sure it looks the part of your industry and make it as professional, fashionable, fun, or relaxing as the products or services your business offers.*

This will also be a great opportunity to do some "Promote Directly" and hand out product samples or promotional items.

Trade Shows

(Also covered in Chapter 15 titled, "How and Where to Get the Products You Want to Sell.")

> *At Trade Shows, manufacturers, distributors, and retailers showcase their existing or future line of products to businesses or consumers.*

Trade shows are frequently opened in major cities across America including but not limited to Las Vegas, New York City, Los Angeles, and Dallas. Research and see which Trade Shows cater to your specific business.

At Trade Shows manufacturers, distributors, and retailers showcase their existing or future line of products to businesses or consumers. It is a great way to connect and communicate with the businesses that provide the products for your industry type. As a retailer, you can view merchandise, negotiate, and place orders for products that you wish to sell.

To determine when and where trade shows in your industry will be taking place; search the Internet for "trade shows _____ (list your business type or industry). The information you need is made available on the search results. Just remember, travel may be required so make sure you factor that into your budget.

 **Tips on Advertising**

The methods mentioned are not the only forms of advertising but they are the most common. Make a decision as to which method or methods to use for your business type and industry. As a new business owner that decision may be very difficult. I suggest you research and learn from other businesses in similar industries and see which advertising methods they utilize.

Once that information is gathered you will have a good starting point.

Learn how to speak to your potential customers in a way that produces results. You have a short time, usually seconds to catch their attention.

INTERACTIVE Which advertising methods are most likely to catch the attention of your potential customers and why?

_____

_____

_____

_____

_____

_____

_____

From Potential Customer to Actual Customer

You must communicate effectively to your potential customers on a level they can understand and relate to.

If your customers are business professionals, farmers, in the construction industry, skate boarders etc., learn their lingo and relate to them.

Example: Have you ever walked into a store designed towards skate boarders? You would almost never see the person behind the counter in a three-piece suit. They will most likely dress and speak similar to their skate boarding customers.

> "Ads get potential customers in the door,
> and then it is your job to turn them into actual customers."

That is the challenge, from potential to actual.

Sometimes customers decide to purchase products or services based on pricing. Other times the decisions are based on the relational skills and personality of the business owner or sales person.

How many times have you become a repeat customer to a business just because you love the personalities of the staff and how you were treated?

All successful restaurants know that it is economical to buy groceries and eat at home. So why do people still choose to dine out? Atmosphere and convenience are the dominating factors.

The restaurant devises a way to make you feel welcome by creating an atmosphere you can relate to and enjoy. They also make a connection with your desire to have that added convenience of letting someone else do the cooking and serving while you sit, relax, and enjoy.

Some restaurants have perfected it, and others still have a long way to go.

 Make it your goal to know how your customers communicate and how you can relate to them. Knowing what they want or expect and provide it for them.

This could take a while to develop and master so do not be discouraged if you are having trouble at first. Just take gradual steps towards achieving your goal.

Direct or Indirect Message

Each of these methods work great for advertising. They are used by leading industry corporations and medium to small businesses.

Direct Message - is promoting exactly what you have to offer whether products or services, along with information on how to contact you. When someone sees your advertisement, they read it and make a determination on whether or not they need your products or services.

Let's use an auto insurance company for example. If you owned an auto insurance business and wanted to advertise directly to your potential customers, you would distribute an advertisement with your business name, phone number, slogan, website, insurance products, and sample rates you offer.

You connect with your audience by directly offering your products and services up front.

Indirect Message - is promoting a topic, subject, or theme while delivering your business as a solution at the end of the promotion. Let's use the same insurance company and instead of a direct message we will use an indirect message to ask a question like the following.

"Is your auto insurance rate too high?" If you do not know the answer to that question, it probably is. Give us a call and we can lower your auto insurance rate today."

Alternatively, your ads could say, "Are you a good driver? If yes, then you deserve the lowest insurance rate possible. Give us a call and we can make sure you get what you deserve.

With an indirect message, you are causing potential customers to read, view, or hear something that they can connect with or answer a question.

Both methods have worked well for companies for many years. The only way to know which one will work for you is to try them both.

 **Exercise**

Think of advertisements that come to mind because they stood out to you in some way and list them.

_____

_____

_____

_____

_____

_____

What made these ads stand out and make you remember them?

_____

_____

_____

_____

How many were direct and how many were indirect?

_____

_____

Next, research and find a few advertisements that are direct, indirect, or both and list them here. You can find them on commercials, print ads, newspapers, or your local advertisements from the mail, etc.

List the company name, industry, what they are advertising, and method used.

_____

_____

_____

_____

_____

_____

What stood out to you about these ads?

_____

_____

_____

_____

How many were direct and how many were indirect?

_____

_____

Now you have an idea of which type of ad stands out to you, whether direct or indirect. You can see where each business chose to place their advertisement, either on a paper ad, commercial etc. Do they effectively reach their target market? Do they offer a fair price on their ads, give you an estimate of the cost, or want you to call them for info? Are their ads clear and to the point or cluttered with too much information?

These are things to consider when placing ads for your business.

Step back and consider which type of ads will stand out to your potential customers.

 ***Note:*** *What stands out to you may not be the same thing that stands out to your customers.*

List some advertising options here for your business:

_____

_____

_____

_____

_____

_____

_____

_____

_____

Communicating Effectively to Your Potential Customers

Think about how you can make a connection with your potential customers, which in turn produces repeat or referral business.

Example: Let's say you own a fitness gym named Triton Fitness Center and you provide a facility where people come and exercise in classes or on their own by using your gym equipment.

Your different ads could say the following:

"Train together, Sweat together, Grow together - Triton Fitness Center" – this ad is tailored to people wishing to add mass to their body. You may want to add a picture of muscular individuals with the ad.

"Train together, Sweat together, Lose Weight together" - Triton Fitness Center" – this ad is tailored to people wishing to lose weight. You may want to add a picture of individuals, "before and after weight loss".

"Need a spotter, we can help – Brotherhood, Triton Fitness Center"

"Triton Fitness Center, where boys become men"

"Attention Ladies - our aerobics instructor's name is Fabio - Enough said - Triton Fitness Center"

"Behind every strong man is a strong woman…about to pass him up. -Ladies of Triton Fitness Center"

"Men & Women of all fitness levels, we offer a step by step program to help you reach your fitness goals. Free childcare available. Couples discount."

Another Example:

Now let's "maximize the gyms business potential" and add a spa to it that offers different types of massages.

The new business name is "Triton Fitness Center & Spa."

Your different ads could say the following:

"Tired? Muscles sore? We can help. Deep tissue massage now available.
   Discount with gym membership"

"Muscles grow during rest. That's where we come in"
   Enjoy our relaxing therapeutic massage right after your workout.

"Workout hard. Relax hard"
   Deep tissue massage available.

"Train. Massage. Repeat"

"Give your muscles a break, they've earned it" Massage service available.

"Ladies night – Relax your mind and body with a Swedish style massage.
   Let's be honest - You deserve it!"

Let's take a few moments and write some examples of ways you can communicate and relate to your target market. It does not have to be perfect or complete just try your best to write some generalized ideas. When it is time to run the advertisements you will consult with the sales department from your advertising method. They generally have ideas on how to tailor your ad toward your target market and since you are running ads with them, graphic design could possibly be free or at a lower cost.

INTERACTIVE List some direct and indirect advertising messages while considering your industry, target market and communicate in a way your customers can relate.

_____

_____

_____

_____

_____

_____

_____

_____

_____

Extremely IMPORTANT Communicating effectively with your customers is extremely important when advertising because you have a limited amount of time to get and keep their attention. You want to make sure that every part of the information counts.

When deciding on advertising methods it is best to consider which ones your customers are likely to view or have an interest. There is always a chance that you have found the perfect advertising method for your company but may need more help with designing the ad. If your advertising method's graphic department came up with the ad, and you are not receiving the response you expected, ask for a redesign. If you still have issues, you may want to consult with a Marketing & Advertising agency for professional assistance. There are upfront costs. However, the benefits of communicating effectively will far outweigh the costs in the end.

Take Surveys, Do Follow-up Calls

You need to know how every customer heard about your business. You can do that by asking them either in person, over the phone during a follow-up call, email, or any other way you communicate with your customers. If you are using several methods of advertising, you will want to know which ones are effective and which ones are not. During a follow-up call, you can suggest other products, services, and get feedback on their experience with your company. It is very important to listen to the positive and negative feedback given to you. This makes it possible to know if your customers are satisfied with your business.

 Remember, you cannot please everyone, but if 90 people out of 100 are complaining about the same thing, you need to make some changes. And if 90 people out of 100 are satisfied then you are on the right track!

Either way, respond to every complaint and try to provide a resolution according to your company policies.

"Your business should always be changing for the better, keeping up with the times, and constantly listening to your customers' positive or negative criticism."

Final Advice

One of the absolute best ways to advertise is to use actual testimonies from real customers who have experienced a great product, service, and remarkable customer service. It is one thing to advertise with clever ads, but to have real customers confirming your ads with a positive testimony, is priceless. I suggest adding customer testimonies throughout your website.

Finding the right method to successfully advertise your business can be a stressful task all in itself, especially if you are new to owning a business. Remember to do as much research as possible for advertising strategies in your industry and try different methods cautiously and in increments. If you have multiple locations in different cities keep in mind that each may require different advertising strategies to reach your target market.

Now that you have completed this chapter, you should know who your target market is, what their habits are, your budget, and several ways to advertise and/or market to your potential customers.

The only thing to do now is to get started!

Chapter 22

Focus on Providing Excellent Products, Services, and Customer Service

*"You can have the recipe for success in your hand but do not forget to
add one more ingredient: Customer Service."*

Let's say you have the perfect marketing strategy that communicates and relates to your target market. Let's say you are able to offer great pricing on your products and services. Let's say you have vast knowledge about your industry and are very passionate about your business. Let's say your business plan is so flawless and rock solid it could be used as an example for others to follow. Your business could still experience a loss by exhibiting poor customer service.

Providing services and customer service is not the same thing. Example: a plumber may be able to service your home and fix every problem, however he may be rude and short tempered.

*One of the major reasons businesses do not receive repeat business
or referrals is "Poor Customer Service."*

On another note, let's say your company offers excellent customer service but your products and services could use some improvement.

Your company will be judged every time a customer interacts with it. Give them a reason to be satisfied on as many categories as possible.

Category	Excellent	Average	Poor
Products			
Services			
Customer Service			
Website			
Location			
Promptness			
Packaging			
Etc.			

Exercise I - Identify Poor Products and Customer Service Experiences

Think about the times you have received a poor product/service or poor customer service from businesses you interacted with. Literally, put this book down and take a few moments to think.

INTERACTIVE   List at least two examples.

_____

_____

_____

_____

List how you felt once you received the poor product/service or poor customer service and if you took any actions. Example: complained to management, filed a formal complaint with the corporate office, told a friend, posted something on social media, decided to not do business anymore with that company or let it all go and give the business or employee another chance.

_____

_____

_____

_____

Would you become a repeat customer? Would you refer your family or friends to that business?

_____

_____

_____

_____

Let's recap.

- The company owner had a plan in place to have a business in existence.

- The company advertised or marketed correctly because they were able to get you in the door.

- The company offered a fair price because you agreed to pay for the products or services.

Consequently, the only problem was either a <u>poor product/service</u> or <u>poor customer service.</u>

Exercise II – Identify Excellent Product, Service and Customer Service Experiences

Let's think of the times you have received an excellent product/service or excellent customer service and were completely satisfied with the results of your interaction with the business.

List at least two examples.

_____

_____

_____

_____

How did you feel afterwards? Would you become a repeat customer? Would you refer your family or friends to that business?

_____

_____

_____

_____

I want you to think about how important it is for you to receive great products, services, and great customer service. Think about how you felt and your actions afterwards, whether positive or negative.

 A company's products, services and level of customer service will determine whether or not you are a repeat customer or if you will refer others. Customers will judge a business by the way they feel when interacting with it.

Use the positive examples you listed as a standard in your own company. Make sure when you hire your employees that they are customer service oriented and are passionate about their position and your products or services.

Remember, after interacting with your customers they will leave with a positive or negative attitude. Make sure you focus on providing excellent products and excellent customer service, then sales will come and your competition will not be able to keep up.

Look at your products or services, is there any way they can be improved?

How about the way they are delivered? Is your packaging high or poor quality? Is there a way to offer it faster or more convenient to your customers? Is there something you can add or take away from your product to make it function better?

_____

_____

_____

_____

How about your offered services, are they up to the quality standards that you would want in receiving services? If yes, then you are doing a great job, keep doing it.

If no, list a few ways you can improve your services.

_____

_____

_____

_____

Customer Service Staff

Next, look at your customer service standards, is your customer service friendly, understanding, patient, and willing to go the extra mile to make your customers happy?

Always staff your customer service with outstanding individuals who really care about making sure your customers have the utmost positive experience.

"Always do your best, always stay focused, and definitely always move forward. "

Final Advice

Without your customers, you would not be in business. So why not do everything you can to make their experience with your company pleasant and enjoyable.

View this chapter as a guideline to work gradually towards; do not expect to have every detail of your business to be in perfect alignment but rather as a work-in-progress that is steadily improving.

Chapter 23

Sales & Negotiating

"Every business should do their best to save money, keep costs low, and sell their products or services at a fair and reasonable price which in turn will produce a profit."

In this chapter, I will go over some basic sales and negotiating methods as well as different options you have when choosing a strategy.

Let's get started with sales.

Sales by definition is the exchange of goods, services, or property for money. (Merriam-Webster)

Every business must conduct sales in order to stay operational. No sales means no business.

List the type of sales your specific business will be making.

- Business to business sales (B2B)

- Business to consumer sales (B2C)

- Or both.

 List here B2B, B2C, or both.

Sales Approach

When approaching your potential customers you want to make sure you have the basics down first.

- ✓ Smile and present yourself appropriately for the industry you are representing.

- ✓ Be confident, knowledgeable and passionate about your products or services.

- ✓ Know pricing and discounts if available for every item you offer.

- ✓ Have examples or testimonies of other satisfied customers.

Next, you will want to determine the level of aggressiveness you want to employ: low, moderate, or high. You are able to try different levels and see which one works best for your business.

Some businesses choose to stick with low or moderate aggressiveness while providing an excellent product at a fair price with exceptional customer service. Being overly aggressive can get you a sale but can cause customers to feel like they were "bullied" or "tricked" and they may not purchase from you again nor provide any referrals. Some B2B companies use the highly aggressive sales approach because of so much competition, the choice is yours to make.

Seven Stages of the Sales Cycle

These general stages are usually directed toward B2B companies, though I will do my best to write it so the concept can be used in any business.

Prospect For Leads

1. If your business is retail or deals with the public in any way, you can design your storefront to attract customers. Run local ads to motivate customers to call you or to come to your place of business.

2. If your business is B2B, you could hire a lead generating company or do your own research and gather a list of businesses that are in your target market for your products or services.

3. If your business is web based you could place several ads on search engines that will generate clicks, which allow potential customers to visit your website.

Regardless of your business type you should conduct social media marketing, have an email campaign, and post online ads.

Set an Appointment

1. If your business is retail or deals with the public, you have set hours that your business is open. Therefore, the general public can stop by to inquire or shop during those hours. You will want to list your phone number for inquires and hours of operation on your advertisements and website.

2. If your business is B2B your job will be to set an appointment with the person who makes decisions (which isn't always the easiest thing to do). You can cold call, do mail outs, email, or stop by and start asking questions. It may take a few visits to establish contact with the right person so keep that in mind.

Qualify the Prospect

This is to confirm that your potential customer is able and has an initial desire to purchase your products or services. Once you have confirmed make your presentation.

Make Your Presentation

1. If your business is retail or deals with the public, you want to showcase your products in a way that is appealing to the eye of your potential clients; or have materials that explain the details and benefits of your services. (Clothing stores do this in the form of mannequins while Spa's do this in the form of brochures.)

2. If your business is B2B, here is where you explain in detail your products or services to the person who makes decisions. This can be done in person or over the phone, hopefully while the decision maker is looking at a catalog or website to get a better idea of what you are selling. Be prepared to give costs and be prepared to negotiate.

3. If you run an Internet based business, your presentation is done on your website in the form of graphics with details or videos that show your products functionality.

Address the Prospect's Objections

As business owners, we usually feel that our products or services are the best and every one should purchase them. However, sometimes our potential customers need additional explanation and persuasion to feel the same way.

With that being said, take some time and think about some of the objections or questions your potential customers may have about your products or services and be ready to give an answer.

Here are a few examples of potential questions you could be asked but will vary depending on the type of business you are in. The answers are only an option or example of how you could respond. You need to determine answers to the questions or objections potential customers could give you concerning your products or services.

> *"Keep in mind that no one likes to be rushed into a decision."*

248

Business to Business

Question: Why should I use your product or service instead of your competitors?

Answer: Although we offer the same products, my company offers a higher level of customer service along with a customer satisfaction guarantee.

Objection: I will have to think about it and will get back to you.

Answer: Sure, no problem that is completely fine. When would be a good time to follow up with you? Are there any other questions I could address to help you in making your decision?

 **Note:** *Keep in mind that no one likes to be rushed into a decision.*

However, you can choose to be aggressive and keep pushing the sale or you can choose to offer a few "extras" to your potential client for making up their mind within a set number of days. "Extras" could be a discount on the product or service, free or discounted shipping, offer an additional item at a discounted rate, etc.

Business to Consumer

Objection: I am interested but will shop around and come back.

Answer 1: No problem we will close around 7 p.m. and if you decide to come back, we will be more than happy to assist you.

Answer 2: That is fine just remember that our sale is for a limited time only.

Answer 3: No problem but if you find a price lower than ours, we will match it to win your business.

Price matching could lower your profits at first but you could gain repeat business. You will need to weigh your options.

Now that you have read a few examples of questions, objections, and answers let's take a moment to consider your specific products or services.

What questions and objections could your potential customers give you and what would your response be?

 *Note: If you are an existing business, you should have experienced questions and objections already.*

If you are a new business start-up, you may need to take some time to consider what questions and objections you may face. If you are having difficulty coming up with a list, ask a few friends or family members for help. Consulting with an outsider to get a different point of view in this area could be particularly beneficial.

Before making sales, you should make sure you have answers or responses ready to give to potential customers.

List questions, objections, and answers here:

_____

_____

_____

_____

_____

_____

_____

_____

_____

_____

_____

_____

Close the Sale

Now it is time to ask for the sale to be complete. Depending on your type of business determines the exact way you communicate with your potential customer to close the sale. Here are a few examples of "closing the sale" tips you can use; simply change the responses to fit your business.

1. You can speak to your customers with an assumption that they have decided to purchase from you, nevertheless, they are thinking about the final details. Example: So which color did you decide to go with? Would you like to have this shipped to you direct or would you like to pick it up?

2. You can use a time limit or a discount close. Example: It is a great choice that you decided to purchase this product today because we may run out of stock and the sale could be over soon. By purchasing today, you will be saving 10% off the suggested retail price.

3. You may choose not to use any particular method and present all of the details of your products or services and let the customer purchase when they decide.

Ask for Referrals

Immediately following a sale is the perfect time to ask for referrals. Your customer is typically excited about their purchase and your excellent customer service and would likely be more than happy to refer someone they know to you. Even if they end up not purchasing from you, I still suggest you ask for a referral. Just because your product or service is not necessary for one person does not mean that is the same for everyone in their lives. You will never know unless you ask. Do not miss this great opportunity.

Keep this mindset: This person could know someone who could use my product or service.

Final Advice on Sales

Whether your business is B2B or B2C, make sure your sales staff is likable. People love interacting with other people that have great attitudes, positive perspectives on life and are overall pleasant individuals. Think of how many times you purchased an item and thought to yourself how much you really liked the attitude of the sales rep. Your sales staff can have all the experience and knowledge in the world, but if they lack likability, it will hinder your sales figures.

When hiring, training, or doing the sales yourself, remember; being likable equals more sales and outstanding customer service. It may take some time to evaluate the sales process that works for your business type. Do not be afraid to try new things or even read other books solely focused on teaching "Sales Strategies."

You may receive several "not interested" answers but keep pushing forward. If you are B2B, while you are going from store to store or business office to business office make sure to keep a positive attitude.

 *Ensure your sales strategy includes a plan to retain existing customers while obtaining new ones.*

Purchase Options for Your Customers

In order to have sales you must have purchase options set in place.

Your purchase options are the different methods your customers can purchase from you. Examples are: in-person sales, a website store, and over the phone sales, etc. There should never be a reason that your customers are not able to buy from you due to a lack of options.

Negotiating

"Negotiating by definition is a strategic discussion that resolves an issue in a way that both parties find acceptable." (Investopedia)

As you start and run your new business, you will find yourself negotiating more and more when it comes to an office and/or retail space, equipment purchases, supplies or resell products, conferring with contractors, hiring employees, advertising costs, and the like.

Conceivably, you will be able to negotiate on the first price given to you; granted that your counter offer will include something that is acceptable to the person or company you are negotiating with. Negotiations start with an initial offer then are usually countered by another offer. Counter offerings will go back and forth until both parties come to an agreement that is mutually beneficial or acceptable to everyone involved.

- Keep in mind while you are negotiating for the best possible deal that the company you are negotiating with is trying to do the same thing.

- Never be afraid to walk away from a deal or shop other suppliers.

- Never let any supplier know they are the last resort.

Negotiating Examples

Let's go over a few negotiating examples then work on a negotiating strategy that will fit your business.

Let's say you are looking for office and/or retail space:

1. Ask the property manager for the minimum monthly or yearly term they are willing to accept for the leased space and the monthly cost.

2. Be sure to ask about new paint, carpet, or different flooring to be included with lease agreement. If you commit to a longer term than their minimum, would they be willing to lower the monthly cost.

3. Always request that the rental rate not increase during the term of your lease. Also, include an option to give the management company a 30-day notice if your business closes, you can be let out of the lease. Some management companies will agree and some may not or counter offer.

Let's say you are purchasing equipment:

1. Ask the sales price for only half of the equipment you actually need. Once you are given that price, you can request a discount if you purchase more equipment.

2. Find another company that offers the same equipment and let each company know that you are comparing prices. You could go for who is cheaper or ask which company will offer discounted or free shipping and installation.

3. If the sales prices are too high for your budget, you could also inquire about leasing options.

Let's say you are purchasing supplies or products to resell:

1. You should always purchase from a company that will give you a price break when ordering multiple supplies or resell products.

2. Find the price point for half of the items you want to purchase, then double the order and see what type of discount they give you for increasing your order.

3. Always ask for free shipping and inquire about a buy-back option. Buy-back means if purchased products do not sell; you have the option to sell them back to the company where purchased. Frequently, you are required to pay a re-stocking fee, then again, better to pay a fee than saddled with unsellable inventory. Remember, never buy in mass quantities unless you have purchase orders to fulfill. If you buy without purchase orders, your products could sit for a while, and tie up operating cash.

Negotiating with Contractors

1. When dealing with contractors always get a minimum of three bids on whatever project you need completed. Not only base your decision on pricing, but on experience and timeliness of completing the job as well.

2. Let all contractors know you are seeking other bids for the same project and ask them for their cost by labor and material. Always have an agreed upon time frame for job completion and have every decision, option, and agreement in writing. Not doing so, could result in ordering incorrect materials and "he said" "she said" arguments.

3. If the bids are similar from each contractor, you can request a discount or extra services they may provide.

4. It is never wise to pay a contractor in full before services are rendered. I suggest pay half up front and half upon completion or pay all after completion if the contractor agrees.

5. If your business provides contract services, always stress the importance of experience, time frame, and any guarantees when submitting your bid.

In some instances when working with contractors the owner of the company may send an employee to perform the work. Once the work is performed the employee may suggest that if you need any further help contact him or her directly for a cheaper price instead of using the company.

I highly suggest you decline the offer although the employee is offering a cheaper price by using them directly. There will be no guarantee or dedicated customer service along with the product or service. The employee may not be available for further assistance and you will have to find another company. Working with dishonest contractor employees may result in a loss when comparing the cost and time spent finding another contractor.

Negotiating Advertising Costs

Once you decide, which advertising options (paper ads, radio, etc.) you want to use, you need to contact several companies that provide these services. Each company will have a set price on their media kits, which is typically negotiable. You may ask for a lower price if you are willing to run your ad for a longer time. It is possible you could go back and forth a few times until you agree on a plan and price that will work for both parties.

Never accept the first price offered, but rather use that as a starting point to negotiate.

You could hire an advertising agency to manage your ad purchasing for you. They generally charge for developing your advertisements and receive a percentage of the amount you spend with the advertiser. Make sure you determine your cost directly from the advertiser then figure your cost using an agency. It may be less expensive, the same, or more expensive to use an agency. Overall, you can decide to use an agency according to cost and the time it will free you up to focus on other aspects of your business. Time is money. Depending on how much the agency works with different advertisers will determine the types of discounts they receive and pass on to you.

Tips on Negotiating

Your actual negotiations will vary depending on your industry and type of business. With the examples given, I hope you have a better understanding of negotiation techniques and are confident in applying these methods toward building and growing your business. Remember, the people you are negotiating with are not your friends, and they want to get the best deal, just like you. Do not be afraid to make counter offers.

- Do your absolute best to keep costs low and make sure you know all your options before signing or agreeing to anything.

- Never be afraid to walk away from a deal if it does not seem right. More often than not, trusting your gut instinct helps you when negotiating.

- Before you start to negotiate, determine exactly the lowest amount you are willing to accept or the highest amount you are willing to pay for the deal in question.

- Negotiating normally refers to the cost amount of a deal; however, it may also be by payment terms or asking for extras like a longer guarantee, free shipping and installation, etc.

Negotiations Your Business Type May Encounter

> *"Never accept the first price offered, but rather use that as a starting point to negotiate."*

Let's take a few moments and think about the types of negotiations your business will likely encounter within the first year.

 List them here. Example: Purchasing office furniture, negotiating advertising and signage costs, etc.

_____

_____

_____

_____

Remember, speak to a few companies that offer the same or similar products or services to compare pricing. I have found that the cheapest price is not always the best product or service offered, nonetheless that is a decision for you to make.

List Companies You Will Negotiate With

Write down a few companies you want to start negotiations with, either now or in the near future. Call them and compare pricing. If you are unsure at this moment, you can come back to this section when you are actually ready to start negotiating. If you are an existing business, you may be prepared to complete this section now, or you can return to it later as well.

_____

_____

_____

_____

_____

Final Advice

There are books, videos, and other writings about sales and negotiating. Do your research and learn all you can about this topic as it will be vital to operating and growing your business.

Never stop learning!

Chapter 24

Maximizing Your Business Potential

"They are already your customers; increase customer satisfaction and sales by offering them additional products or services."

A strategy I call "Maximizing Your Business Potential" is about looking beyond your initial products and services and thinking of other things you can offer your existing customers based on their needs and interests. It is also thinking outside the box and figuring out creative ways to sell your existing products or services that are currently not selling too well. In doing so, you will not only expand your customer base by providing extra products or services but will also increase sales and thus increase profits.

For example, I will use a global company that most may be familiar with, "AT&T".

They are commonly known for offering home phone and cell phone service. As of now, in most areas they offer cable TV, Internet services and home security systems. They did not begin their business by offering cable, Internet and home security; although, eventually they maximized their business potential by adding those extra services and offering them to their new and existing customers. (AT&T)

Offering Additional Products and Services

The basic idea is asking yourself this question—

> *What else can I offer my customers that could be useful to them without having to start a brand new business?*

Your customers are already purchasing from you so you could capitalize on the opportunity to offer them additional products or services.

I have listed a few business types and maximized their potential in a couple of ways so you can get a better idea of what it means and apply the concept to your own business.

<u>Restaurant</u> – you currently offer food, drinks, dessert, and great customer service.

Maximized Potential

- Start a catering division and reach out to local businesses, weddings, holiday office parties, local organizations who gather for meetings.

- If your desserts are not selling well, you can start packaging some as "To Go" items and offering them as an "add on" while taking their original order. On average, many customers may be too full after their meal to order dessert. If they knew, purchasing it to go is an option, and they could enjoy that treat later, you might make more dessert sales.

- Instead of selling individual menu items, start offering popular items as package deals. For instance, you can offer appetizers for two, entrées for two, and a shared dessert for a set package price.

- You can start offering extra toppings that compliment your meal.

- You can offer a giant-sized burger, steak, or other popular items and have your customer see if they can finish the whole meal within a specific time. As a reward, you can offer it for half price if they win. It is a fun challenge, and brings added excitement to the table and surrounding tables, providing you present it uniquely. As a benefit for you, your customers may take pictures and post them on their social media accounts, giving your business free advertisement.

> *What else can I offer my customers that could be useful to them without having to start a brand new business?*

Clothing Retail Store – you currently offer clothes, shoes, accessories for children and teens.

Maximized Potential

- Start an online clothing store offering free shipping on orders over a certain amount.

- Start an ebay.com store to get more business exposure with the capability to reach customers all across the U.S.

- Offer tailoring services.

- Research the opportunity to offer uniforms for your local or nearby school's athletics, dance, band, and drama departments.

- Locate other businesses that cater to children or teens and offer to produce their employee uniforms.

- Partner with a dry-cleaning service.

Furniture Store – you currently offer home, office, and/or patio furniture.

Maximized Potential

- Offer a home or office moving service.

- You could partner with a contractor that works on homes or offices to provide remodeling, painting or repair services, carpet or wood flooring sales and installation.

- You could partner with a company that offers residential alarm equipment and services.

- You could purchase (in bulk) chairs, tables, and fixtures and rent them for parties or events.

Accounting Office – you offer accounting services for small to medium-sized businesses.

Maximized Potential

- You could offer payroll services.

- You could offer printing services.

- Small business owners may need a part-time receptionist or administrative assistant to help answer calls while they are busy with clients. They could take messages and book appointments for them.

- You could brand your business name and open more locations. Then hire accountants to handle those locations.

These are just a few business types with examples of how to maximize their business potential.

Your job is to take the basic concept and apply it to your own business.

Final Advice

Do not try to do everything at once. You first need to test concepts and see whether they will be profitable for your business. Do not try to add a new concept to your business just because you see someone else doing it. That is a huge mistake and it could cost you lots of money. I cannot express the numerous times people have tried to copy someone else's business idea and failed. Make sure you have some original creativity and knowledge about the concept that you are going to add to your business.

"Success usually comes to those who have <u>passion</u>, <u>patience</u>, <u>persistence</u>, and a well thought out <u>plan</u>, not just a desire to make money".

 *Note: View this chapter as guidelines to work towards gradually; do not expect to have every detail of your business in perfect alignment but rather as a work-in-progress that is steadily improving. No business is perfect at any stage they are in. Always do your best, always stay focused, and definitely always move forward.*

Chapter 25

Administration, Accounting, and Budgeting

"Day-to-Day Operations"

This chapter covers basic day-to-day and monthly operations for your business.

If you do not have employees be sure to schedule time to handle these operations. If you have employees you may split administration and accounting duties among your staff, do it yourself, or outsource it. Either way, the decision should be based on your business operations and cash flow. If you have a strong background in a specific business operation, you might consider taking on the task to save on costs.

Let's get started with Administration.

Administration

Administration by definition is the day-to-day process or activity of running a business or organization. (Bing)

Administration for your small business includes but not limited to:

- Answering phones.

- Ordering supplies.

- Keeping up with inventory.

- Scheduling employee hours and meetings.

- Secretarial work – faxing, filing, emails, etc.

- Handling incoming and outgoing mail.

Example

Let's say you own a small local coffee shop.

You have employees serving coffee to customers, employees who clean up after customers, and a manager to manage the shop. There are several behind the scene duties that come into play before the coffee can to get into the hands of customers.

Administrative functions might be ordering coffee from suppliers, ordering cups and lids, ordering cleaning supplies, answering phones, handling paperwork, faxing or filing, etc. Essentially, it is the "back office" stuff, which requires handling in order for your business to operate day by day. You can also add bill payments, which are considered light accounting and can be handled by an administrative position.

List Your Day-To-Day Administration Operations

INTERACTIVE Take some time and think about the various administrative duties your type of business will require for day-to-day operations.

_____

_____

_____

_____

Next, determine whether you want to assume the duties, let your employees do them along with their other tasks, or hire someone specifically for administration.

Accounting

Accounting by definition is the action or process of keeping financial accounts. (Google)

Small business accounting includes:

- Managing business expenses.
- Producing invoices.
- Making bill payments.
- Posting payments.
- Managing financial reports.
- Budgeting.
- Profit/loss statements.
- Quarterly tax reporting and yearly tax filing.

Accounting Software

Intuit QuickBooks® is a great software tool to use for managing the accounting tasks for your small business. I find them to be cost-effective and user friendly. It requires investing some time to learn its functions; overall, I highly recommend using the software. There are other accounting software programs. Do your research and find one that meets your specific business needs according to your industry type.

Simply go to the Internet, type "small business accounting software for _____" (list your industry).

Note: Make sure your accounting software is tailored to your industry type and do not spend too much on your first purchase. As your business grows, so will your software needs, so make sure your software has the capability to grow with your business or at least transfer your existing data to another software. I have found that most accounting software programs can transfer data to an Microsoft Excel spreadsheet then you can upload that data to another accounting software when necessary.

If you are going to use the same software to run your business and accounting operations, ensure you have separate accounts or passwords. If you hire employees, you may not want certain positions to have access to your accounting reports.

In addition, while operating your small business my recommendation is to contract a CPA or Accountant to manage your monthly profit/loss reports, quarterly federal tax filings, and year-end tax filing. That is unless your small business is an accounting firm; you should be able to do the work yourself just fine. However, for the rest of us, this suggestion helps you see on a monthly basis where your business stands as far as expenses and profits. You will not have to worry about missing important filing dates and run your business free from filing hassles.

Budgeting

A budget by definition is an estimation of the revenue and expenses expected over a given period in the future. (Dictionary)

Budgeting is a very important aspect within your company. It helps determines whether you have enough funds to meet or exceed your expenses.

First, take an account of how much cash is available to invest in your business. Cash can come from your own personal finances, from partners, or investors, and the like. Then write either a list, spreadsheet, bullet point, or graph (depending on how technical you are) of all the start-up costs, if applicable, and at least three to six months of expenses, you will incur while operating your business.

Examples of Generic Expenses

Your type of business will determine your costs.

There are start-up costs and monthly costs that you will need to factor in your budget.

Listed are some generic expense categories that just about every business incurs:

- Business registration, permits, licensing.

- Graphic design for logo, advertisements, business cards, letterhead, envelopes, etc.

- Signage and advertisement materials – business cards, brochures, etc.

- Office or retail location costs, security deposit, etc.

- General office supplies – computer, desk, chairs, printer, etc.

- Utility services - most office buildings and malls include utilities within your monthly rental fee. Retail locations for the most part, do not.

- Website registration, hosting, & development.

- Inventory of products you will sell.

- Business equipment.

- Commercial insurance.

- Any other start-up plus six month costs your new business may have.

List as many other start-up costs, if applicable, and monthly expenses you can think of for your business.

It is common to include three to six months of monthly expenses in your final number. Once sales are made, factor your revenue into your budget.

Revenue is the amount of money your company receives during a specific amount of time.

Depending on your expenses and revenue, your budget will fall into one of these three categories.

- Surplus budget – a profit is expected.

- Balanced budget – revenues are expected to equal expenses.

- Deficit budget – expenses will exceed revenue.

 When calculating your budget make sure to take into account how much it costs to purchase or produce the products you are selling. Make sure it also includes future expenses.

Example - Let's say your business has $5,000 in profit from sales. Next month's bills are $2,000 so budgeting will help you realize that you have enough cash to cover them.

When it is time to hire employees, you can use budgeting to determine how much you can afford to pay them while *making sure you have enough to pay expenses and yourself.* It will help you balance how much money you currently have, and how much you will spend in the near future.

Chapter 26

Understanding Your Role in Your Company

"Position yourself to succeed."

This chapter is for you if:

- Your business has employees.

- Your business is about to hire employees.

- You want to outsource some business tasks.

This chapter gives you an understanding of the role you play within your own company and helps you position employees, so they can excel in their area of expertise.

 *Note: There are many other positions. I am listing the basics for general business.*

Basic Positions in General Business

- Founder, President, Chief Executive Officer, General Manager, Managing Member, Director, Officer Etc.

- Sales And Marketing Team.

- Advertising Team.

- Graphic / Web Design Team.

- Creative & Product Development.

- Buyers or Purchasing Department.

- Accounting.

- Legal.

- Administrative Assistants.

- General Laborers.

- Operations Manager.

- General Retail or Office Staff.

If you do not have employees yet, then you will be responsible for every role in your company. This is sometimes challenging but exactly how several successful companies have started.

If you have employees, your role within your company will mean more than just a title.

- You will be the leader for every employee to follow, so make sure to lead by example.

- Your staff will look to you for direction and a strategy to reach company goals.

- Your attitude (whether positive or negative) will be an example for your employees to follow.

- You will be in charge of making sure your company culture is practiced among your employees and customers.

- You will be the one who has to make the tough choices and have the final say.

- You will be in charge of your company's growth.

Also, as the owner of your company, you should always hold the highest level of authority plus any other position you choose to manage.

 *"Never be afraid to hire someone smarter than you are in a specific area, their expertise could be the answer to your company's growth"*

When hiring you need to place people in positions where they fully utilize their skills and abilities. Discover their expertise and let them excel in that position.

For example, I have found that hiring individuals with years of sales experience has paid off tremendously more than me trying to be the lead sales person.

In addition, I do not possess experience in graphic or web design nor do I have the time to learn. First, I outsourced and later hired a graphic/web design team to handle everything I need in that area.

I have experience in creative process and product development as well as some areas of accounting. I chose to continue handling portions of these daily tasks.

The basic idea is not to be so caught up in the mindset, that you feel obligated to handle every role within your company just because you are the owner.

Many effective business owners have succeeded because they were not afraid to hire people that are able to excel in an area that they, themselves, may have been limited.

If your goals are customer satisfaction and company growth, placing the right people in the right positions will be the key to making that happen.

I always say, "Let the pros handle what they went to school for and learned to handle."

Look at your vehicle for a moment, it is likely you did not build it from raw materials nor program its functions. (If you did I notably commend you for that.) Someone else with expertise in their field built the frame while someone else furnished the inside, someone else programmed its functions while someone else built the engine and so on, and finally, someone else put it all together. You purchased the vehicle and you enjoy its benefits.

Big car makers understand the importance of placing people with expertise in key positions to fulfill a business function, so let's learn from their example.

List Your Company's Roles and Business Functions

Take a moment and list the roles and business functions you will handle then list the ones you will hire employees to handle or outsource.

List the roles and business functions you will handle.

_____

_____

_____

_____

_____

List the roles and business functions you will hire employees to handle or outsource.

_____

_____

_____

_____

_____

_____

By reading this chapter, you now have a greater understanding of the importance of placing the right people in the right positions, as well as what roles you will handle within your company.

Chapter 27

Inventory and Tracking

"You should have a record of every item and know its current value."

Business owners will eventually accumulate product inventory, office equipment, furniture, etc.

For example, if you own an office or retail store you will need desks, store racks, computers, printers, labeling machines, paper supplies, packaging supplies, first-aid kits, fire extinguishers, office chairs, the list can go on.

You should have a record of every item (furniture, products, office supplies, etc.) you own and know its current value along with a tracking system (Excel spreadsheet) so you know where everything is located.

Know the Value of Your Inventory and Equipment

Knowing the value of your inventory and equipment is necessary when filing your yearly local business taxes. You may have to pay a yearly tax to your local governing authority and school district on the value of your items, including inventory. The total item value and business location determines how much you pay. Do not be alarmed, customarily it is not that much compared to what you own. You are able to protest the assessment value amount if you feel that you are being over charged.

Track Your Products

You will need a "system" in place to help track your product inventory. Be certain your system is able to track the products you are buying, shipping costs, how much you are selling them for, which items are sold, which items are still in inventory, and any shipping costs related to delivering the products to your customers.

System - refers to a process in which you are able to accomplish the tasks mentioned. Whether that system is computer software or hand written lists, make sure it is accurate and complete.

For example, if you own a specialty luggage store you will order products to sell from a company that makes specialty luggage.

Here is how the process works:

1. Order the product and give your supplier a PO number.

2. Get the shipping rate and approximate receiving date.

3. Receive product by matching it to the PO and adding it to your existing inventory.

4. Add your pricing to the product.

5. Store products in inventory or display products to sell (you may also have a "for display only" item).

6. After a customer purchases, distribute to customer directly or ship product to customer.

PO stands for purchase order and can be any number you wish to give your supplier as a reference, so when you receive the products you can make sure what you receive is exactly what you ordered. Say you order five blue luggage sets and six red luggage sets then your PO number could be 5B6R and the date you placed the order (5B6R022714). If you are using an inventory tracking software, it should generate a PO number for you or you can make up your own.

You should know exactly where your products are and how many you have available to sell.

Tracking your inventory is the only way you will know when and what items are selling, when it is time to order more products and it helps determine if any items have been stolen.

Track Your Services

If you are in the service industry, you will need to have a system that will help track your services as they are rendered to your customers. Your system should be able to break down different services and discounts. It should indicate when services are expected to be rendered and length of time for the services.

You should be able to schedule an appointment as well as take payments. Your software should be able to store customer information and print out detailed reports. Tracking your customers is essential, especially in a service business.

In general, you will want software that helps you track every step of what has been explained in this chapter.

Conduct an Internet search for "software for _____ (list your business type), and you will have plenty of choices to go through.

You also need to determine how much you are willing to invest on securing the right software.

Alternative To Installed Software

An alternative to purchasing and installing software on your computer is purchasing a monthly license from software companies, which allow your information to be stored on their servers. With a user name and password, you are able to access your information on any computer with an Internet connection. All of your customers' data and your business information will be updated simultaneously, as you conduct business using software provided by these companies on supplied websites.

Installed Software

- You own the software licensing upon purchase.

- Normally the software can be installed on one or more computers.

- Will need a network system in place to have multiple computers updated simultaneously.

- Usually covers 1-3 employees, in some cases you will need to purchase additional licenses to add more users.

- You will need to install updates as they become available.

- If you wish to upgrade you will need to purchase the newer version, sometimes at a discount because you are upgrading and not requiring a complete new install.

Month-to-Month License

- You never own the software as it is more of a lease.

- You are able to access your business or customers' information on any computer with an Internet connection. No need for a network system.

- The amount of users you require will usually determine your monthly fee.

- Your monthly fee will usually cover a small set of users. The cost for additional users will be added to your monthly fees.

- No need to install updates as they will be made automatically.

Final Advice

When I first started in business, I used a Microsoft Excel spreadsheet, which worked fine until my business grew. I then transferred all my existing data into installed software that could handle my customers' information, sales, shipping, accounting, and any other task my business required. When the total number of customers exceeded the capability of my installed software, I transferred over to a month-to-month license with the ability to handle unlimited customers.

In the beginning stages of your business, try not to invest too much money into your software (unless absolutely necessary). Rather, choose one that fits your current needs and possibly two stages of anticipated business growth. Stages of anticipated growth could be multiple locations or the ability for your software to handle several thousand customers.

Whether you choose installed or month-to-month make sure it comes with technical support and a function that will allow you to produce reports to track every area of your business.

Chapter 28

Branding

"Distinguish your business and products from others in the market"

Branding is the process of adding a symbol, mark, logo, name, word, sentence or a combination of these to your business, its products, and advertisements. (Investopedia) Every time your logo, symbol, mark or a product of your company is in the public eye; you have your "branding process" in operation.

Branding can also relate to atmosphere, culture and favorable environments. Customers return for the feeling they experience when purchasing and using your products, eating your food, or shopping in your store. It also gives your business a unique feel and look that customers can recognize and remember.

Examples:

> At Bass Pro Shops customers feel the great outdoors, while enjoying the ambiance of life in the wild.
>
> At Trader Vic's customers experience an Polynesian Island atmosphere and meal.
>
> At Urban Outfitters customers listen to a DJ as they shop for clothing.

Branding is not used in every business and it is completely up to you if you want to use it for yours. I would suggest, however, that you at least use a logo or your business name written with unique characters as your logo and choose a specific set of colors for your business and remain consistent. I definitely suggest using branding techniques if you are a business that deals directly with the public and have or will have multiple locations.

 *Note: This chapter will touch the surface and give you the basics with regards to branding.*

Branding Your Company

Every business should have a set of colors that they use for their logo, signage, letterhead, notices, sales receipts, product packaging, etc. Doing this gives your customers a professional and branded feel they are used to seeing when dealing with major companies.

As you visit stores, restaurants, and so on, look around at the choices made concerning color, decorations, and the overall feel. Ordinarily, when you visit a restaurant that is correctly branded you should be able to visit that same restaurant in a different location or city, and it looks precisely the same as the one you are used to visiting. You should also be able to expect the same level of customer service, quality of products, and overall customer experience.

Branding should be accomplished by asking yourself how you want to be viewed in the public eye. Do you want your business to be viewed as fun and outgoing, relaxed, serious, etc.?

Once you have answered that question, base the overall appearance of your company on it.

Color Schemes

Essentially, when you choose your color scheme your paperwork, logo, contracts, letterhead, website, social media, office appearance, printed handouts, etc. should reflect the same scheme. This gives a familiar feeling to customers as they conduct business with you.

Logo Placement

Your logo should be placed everywhere. On all notices, receipts, business cards, advertising materials, etc. Make sure your logo is consistent with the colors you chose and is placed in areas that customers can easily view. Let your logo reflect the type of business you want to portray to the public. If fun and outgoing, then have a fun and outgoing logo and such.

Be Consistent

You are creating a company in which you want the public to view you as trustworthy, dependent, and reliable. Be certain you continue to exhibit those qualities throughout your business. Let your brand reflect those qualities and be consistent when delivering the best customer experience as possible.

Branding Your Products

Branding your products is similar; except you put into service a large marketing campaign that exposes your logo and product name. Thus, potential customers develop a sense of familiarity. By the time your products are in the stores or on the Internet, customers already have a sense of identification with your company and recognizes its products.

Some businesses choose a logo to market as their brand image and some businesses choose their business name to market for their brand.

For instance, Nike uses a swoosh check-mark as their logo. (Logos) They put that swoosh check-mark on any product and we all know that it is Nike who is marketing that product.

Macy's for example uses their business name to market their business. (Macy's)

Wherever you see the Macy's name, you know it is a large department store in several malls across the country.

 *List Your Business Color Options*

Take a few minutes and list a few color options you would like to use in your business. This determines the color scheme that identifies your business and affixes to all products, media and advertising you produce.

_____

_____

_____

_____

_____

You can use these colors together or try each one at a time to see which one or group of colors fits your business best. If you are design savvy, you can create a few graphic designs for your business. If not, hiring a graphic designer will be the best option to create branding options for your business location, its products, and the overall company look.

For examples and ideas go out in your city and note the differences between branded and non-branded businesses and products. Visit stores that have multiple locations and note the similarities or differences.

 Visit SmallBusinessAA.com for more information concerning Business Registration, Website Development & Online Store, Domain Name (website name), Business Email, Credit Card Processing, Graphic Design & Advertising Materials.

Final Advice

Being consistent with your promises, quality of products, levels of service, and overall customer experience.

Chapter 29

Trademarks, Copyrights, Inventions, & Patents

"Protection for your business name, products, work and inventions."

This chapter is for business owners who wish to file with the appropriate government agency concerning protection of their business name, product name, written work, creation of a new product, etc. We will go over each topic providing definitions and explanations.

Trademarks

Trademark by definition is any <u>name</u>, symbol, figure, letter, <u>word</u>, or <u>mark</u> adopted and used by a manufacturer or merchant in order to designate his or her goods and to distinguish them from those manufactured or sold by others. (Dictionary) Trademarks are registered with the Patent and Trademark Office to assure its exclusive use by its owner.

If you are in the product business and you develop a product that will be in stores, your product's name should be trademarked. Therefore, no one else can use that product name within the industry of your product. It protects you against anyone else using your product name for his or her products in your industry. You may also want to consider trademarking your business name according to the industry you are in.

Trademarked name, logos, etc. are registered within your specific industry.

Let's use the name ABCthirst™, let's say ABCthirst is a water filtration system. You would file a trademark for ABCthirst under the category of water filtration systems. Someone else might use that name on wristbands or T-shirts, then they will have to file a trademark for ABCthirst under clothing and accessories. Since there are so many categories, you must choose one (or more) that is specific for your business industry. If your product name is already registered by someone else in the same industry, then you are not able to use that name.

- The ® means that a trademark has been registered, filed, and approved.

- The ™ means that you have filed for a trademark and are pending approval.

If your application is rejected you are no longer able to use ™ on your products.

In order for your application to be considered for approval, you must be actively using your trademark and conducting business.

It is extremely important to conduct research on availability as it will be very costly and time-consuming to fabricate products and find out later that your product name has been previously trademarked.

Trademarks are not only for products.

Let's say you had a marketing firm called "Market Corp Plus." If you choose, you can trademark your business name under services for marketing, because it is not an actual product.

The trademark office will want to see a photo of "Market Corp Plus" being actively used on an advertising or marketing piece and confirm that the business name is currently being used.

I suggest you do not place large orders of anything you wish to trademark unless you have received an approval by email or by mail.

Copyrights

Copyright by definition is the exclusive <u>right</u> to make <u>copies</u>, license, and otherwise exploit a literary, musical, or artistic work, whether printed, audio, video, etc.: works granted such <u>right</u> by law on or after January 1, 1978, are protected for the lifetime of the author or creator and for a period of 50 years after his or her death. (Dictionary)

Explained – Copyrights generally pertain to written, artistic, audio or video work. The written work you are reading whether it is in the form of a manual, book, or online has a copyright.

If your business produces written, artistic, audio, or video work that is made available to the public, you would definitely want it to have a copyright filed with the U.S. Copyright Office.

Although, if you are able to prove that you were the first person or business to create the work you officially do not have to file a copyright. As soon as your work is out in the public, it automatically becomes your copyright. If someone copies your work, without your express written permission, you can file a lawsuit against them. You must have proof the work was yours first if you intend to go to court.

To remove any doubts I suggest you file your work with the U.S. Copyright Office directly.

Inventions & Patents

To invent by definition is to originate or create as a product of one's own ingenuity, experimentation, or contrivance: To produce or create with the imagination. (Dictionary)

Invention – A new, useful process, machine, improvement, etc., that did not exist previously and that is recognized as the product of some unique intuition or genius, as distinguished from ordinary mechanical skill or craftsmanship. Anything invented or devised. (Dictionary)

In short, an invention is something you create that no one else has.

Inventions have played a major role in what we use today on a normal basis.

We are able to drive cars, turn on lights, use telephones, travel by airplane and it all can be traced to inventors that created or improved something that was not available at that time.

If you feel you have an invention, you will definitely want to file a patent as soon as possible to protect it.

Patents

There are three types of patents according to the USPTO (United States Patent & Trademark Office). We will be discussing the two main patents; utility and design.

Patent - Is is the exclusive right granted by a government to an inventory to manufacture, to use, or sell an invention for a certain number of years. An invention or process protected by this right. (Dictionary)

Patent is a document granted by the government to whoever invented the product; which, allows them to sell their product or design without the worry someone else is copying their invention.

Utility patents cover the majority of patents because it deals with an actual object/product and it protects the function of the item.

Design patents deal with the ornamental (outward appearance) design of a product and not the function.

If you feel that you have an invention that is not out in the market, first hire a professional to do a patent search to make sure no one else has invented the same product or design. You can do so by hiring an attorney or using a patent filing service. The attorney or filing service will advise you of your options once the research is completed.

Chapter 30

Taxes, Expenses, and Business Insurance

"Fundamentals of business taxes, expenses, and business insurance options."

Taxes

While operating your business you will need to stay in compliance with all of the taxes your federal, state or local government require from you.

For example,

- If you sell products and certain services, you need to file sales taxes.

- Depending on where and which type of business you operate, you may need to pay business or personal property tax.

- Depending on the state where you conduct business and the type of entity you chose; you may or may not have to pay yearly franchise tax.

- All businesses that make a profit will have to pay Federal income tax. For example, if your business makes $100,000 a year and has $70,000 in expenses you will only have to pay federal income taxes on $30,000.

- Based on the type of entity you chose, you would have to pay Social Security and Medicare Tax through your business or from the salary, you pay yourself.

Sales Tax – A tax imposed by the government at the point of sale on retail goods and services. It is collected by the retailer and passed on to the state. (Investopedia)

Business Property Tax- If your business owns real property, you must pay property tax. **Real property** is property that includes land and buildings, and anything affixed to the land. For a business, real property would include warehouses, factories, offices, and other buildings owned by the business. Real property only includes those structures that are affixed to the land, not those which can be removed, such as equipment. (biztaxlaw.about.com)

Personal Property Tax- Personal property is property owned by an individual or business which is movable and is not affixed to or associated with the land. Personal property for a business would include equipment, office furniture, cars/trucks purchased and used by the business. (Biztaxlaw.about.com)

Franchise Tax- A franchise tax is charged by a state to corporations and other business entities (LLCs in some states), for the privilege of incorporating or doing business in that state. The franchise tax may be based on income or it may be an annual fee. (Biztaxlaw.about.com)

Federal Income Tax- A tax levied by the United States Internal Revenue Service (IRS) on the annual earnings of individuals, corporations, trusts and other legal entities. (Investopedia.com)

Social Security -The tax levied on both employers and employees used to fund the Social Security program. Social Security tax is usually collected in the form of payroll tax or self-employment tax. (Investopedia.com)

Medicare Tax- the Medicare tax is used to fund the government's Medicare program, which provides subsidized healthcare and hospital insurance benefits to retirees and the disabled. Medicare and Social Security taxes are levied on both employees and employers. (Investopedia.com)

Depending on the state you live in and type of business you operate, determines which other taxes you will be required to pay.

Expenses

Expenses are the monthly costs that you have to pay in order to operate your business.

Here is a list of the most common expenses.

- Business Registration, Permits, Licensing.

- Graphic Design of Logo, Advertisements, Stationary, Etc.

- Signage and Advertisement Materials – Business Cards, Brochures, Etc.

- Office, Kiosk, or Retail Space Monthly Rent.

- Advertising Costs – Print Media, Ads, Radio, TV Commercial, Etc.

- Printing Costs.

- Phone Costs – Equipment And Monthly Fees.

- Travel Costs- Hotel, Meals, Gas, Rental Cars, Airline Tickets, Etc.

- Resale Products and Supplies.

- General Office Supplies – Computer, Desk, Chairs, Printer, Etc.

- Office Furniture or Equipment.

- Payroll Costs.

- Employee Costs.

- Contractor Costs.

- Attorney and CPA Fees.

- Vehicle Costs.

- Parking and Toll Fees.

- Meals and Entertainment.

- Website Registration, Hosting, & Development.

- Purchase of Products Your Business Will Sell.

- Commercial Insurance.

There may be more or less expenses depending on your business type.

 *You should keep all receipts and make purchases with a check or bankcard so there are records of your expenses on monthly bank statements.*

The cost of your expenses will be deducted from the total sales you make for federal income tax purposes. As always, look for less expensive ways to operate your business.

Business Insurance

Business insurance protects your investment by minimizing any financial risk associated with unexpected events such as a lawsuit, fire damage or theft.

There are several types of insurance policies but the most common is called "General Liability."

Purchasing at least a "general liability policy" for any business is usually required if you are going to operate from a storefront, kiosk, office building, etc. Your business type determines the kind or classifications of policies you need and the amount of coverage required. An insurance agent will help you determine which policies are best suited for you.

Having a business insurance policy can protect your company from paying out large sums of money if someone files a lawsuit against your business. Reasons could range anywhere from falling and injuring themselves at your place of business to getting hurt or sick because of a product you sold them. It could cover your company if fire, theft, or water damage occurs to your products, equipment, or place of business.

If you work out of your home, in some cases you are not required to have an insurance policy; providing your current homeowners' insurance policy covers your business equipment and products from any type of damage or loss. If not, I suggest you purchase a policy to make sure your business is covered. Keep in mind that your homeowners' policy may cover your equipment and products but may not cover your business if someone were to file a lawsuit.

If you own any type of contract labor or tech service company, you need an insurance policy to cover you while working at commercial or residential properties.

If you own a store, kiosk, or office space before you move in you may be required to procure at least minimum general liability insurance.

If you operate under a DBA / Assumed Name, I suggest acquiring general liability insurance. If you do not and are in a lawsuit and do not have the cash on hand to pay the damages, your personal possessions may be considered as means to pay what you owe.

If you operate an LLC, or Inc. and do not acquire a general liability policy and do not have the cash on hand to pay the damages from the lawsuit; the courts, in some cases, cannot go after your personal possessions but can cause your company to go into bankruptcy.

I cannot stress the extreme importance of being fully covered with commercial insurance while your business is in operation. The cost is minimal when compared to what you could be facing if you were to suffer a loss or lawsuit and do not have the cash to recoup your losses.

Shop around to determine which policy and insurance company will best fit your business needs and budget.

Chapter 31

Day 1 Grand Opening

Today is your big day!

Checklist

You have made it! Today marks the beginning of your successful journey in entrepreneurship.

Remember, it is OK to feel a little nervous at this point, all new business owners have felt that way.

Let's go over a checklist and overview to ensure you have everything in order.

 *Note: The checklist is not in any specific order and all items listed may not pertain to your business type.*

Let's start by checking off everything you have accomplished so far.

Positive Mindset – stay positive, stay focused. Remember why you wanted to start a business. Focus on your goals and take steps towards them. Constantly remember the victories and success stories you have experienced in your past and know great things are ahead. If you do not have any victories or success stories, then read about others and find out what they did to experience success.

Business Type – make sure you are passionate about your business. If you already have extensive knowledge and experience within your business type, you are ahead of the game, will avoid several costly mistakes, and know what it takes to operate the business. If you do not have knowledge about your business type, then take some time to gain knowledge before stepping out. If you do not have experience in your business type, try working for a similar company to gain valuable experience.

Another option is to find someone who has experience and partner or use them as an advisor. Passion, knowledge, and experience in a business do not always equal profits. You will also need a well thought out plan and a strategy to execute it.

Business Name – Coming up with the perfect name for your business may take some time and careful consideration. While you are deciding on a business name make sure that it is;

- Easy to spell and pronounce
- Available for registration with your county or state
- Available for registration on the Internet
  - Domain name
  - Facebook
  - Twitter
  - Etc.

Business Plan – Make sure to have your business plan ready to present to financial institutions. Know the plan details and present it with confidence.

Plan and Strategy – Develop a plan & strategy that you will follow. It should include the topics listed on this checklist and how you will execute them.

Logo – Design a logo that reflects your company or what your company offers. You can also use your business name as your logo.

Slogan – Make it short and to the point. You can write what you offer or something catchy to get your customers' attention ensuring they remember you.

Color Scheme – Choose one or a set of colors that work well together and use them for advertising materials, packaging, website, office decor, etc.

Graphics – Most business owners choose to have a graphic designer develop the graphics for their business name, website, and advertising materials, etc. Some business owners choose to do the graphics themselves.

Advertising Materials – You will need to have different advertising materials in place to hand out, mail, or display to your potential or actual customers. Business cards, brochures, fliers, post cards, etc.

Business Supplies – Most businesses need at minimum a computer, printer, ink, telephone, fax, pens, paper, staple, etc. Determine what items you will need to perform daily tasks and have them accessible to you and your employees.

Domain Name Registered – Make sure you have a domain name registered for your business. Remember to register multiple extensions (.com, .org, .net) so no one else can register them. You can also register a domain name that is different than your business name yet easy for people to remember.

Website – Once your domain name is registered you will need a website developed. Depending on your business type you may also want to have a website store to sell your products and services. Your website should consist of your business information, products, services, contact information, pricing, photos, testimonials, and any other information or graphics you wish to relay to your customers.

Social Media – Your business should be registered on the different social media platforms that your potential customers are most likely to use. Make sure to update your social media pages regularly with sales, promotions, and other information you wish to relay to your customers.

Hours of Operation – Determine the hours you are able to service your customers. Make sure to post them on the front door of your business, website, and record them on your voice-mail.

Policies – It is very important to have policies in place, so that you will know how to handle situations that may arise with customers and employees.

Your policies may change or be updated as you operate and you will determine which is the best policy for you and your customers to follow. Make sure to give a copy of your policies & agreements to your customers and employees.

Disclaimers – Make sure to let your customers know your guarantees and what you are and are not liable for concerning your products and services.

Credit Card Processing – A majority of consumers use their debit or credit card to make purchases. Be sure you are able to accept card payments in person, over the phone, or on your website.

 *Note: If your business deals with other businesses (B2B) and the cost for your products or services are very high you may want to consider accepting checks to save on the card processing fees.*

Products – Ensure you have negotiated and received the lowest price from your suppliers to purchase the products you wish to sell. Constantly run "sales" or discounts as customers always love a good deal. Make sure your products are on display and ready for purchase.

Services – List your services and price them according to the average market rate. You can offer discounts for new customers or charge above-average rates because of the higher level of outstanding service and/or quicker completion time. Be sure to let your customers know what to expect as a result of your services. They should sign a form or waiver agreeing to the terms of service and price. Your business type will determine whether you should ask for full or half payment upfront or payment due after services rendered.

Advertising Strategy – Determine which advertising methods your customers are most likely to view and respond to. You should start advertising and posting on social media at least one month before your opening day. This will let people know your products or services will soon be available. Collect email addresses so you can send updates about your business. Communicate with your potential customers in a way that they are able to relate to and respond.

Sales Scripts – Have sales scripts available for you and your sales team as a reference when making sales pitches. Do not read word for word; try to make your sales pitch sound natural and confident. Be ready with pricing details and your negotiating limits, if applicable. Always have discounts, specials, or sales with a beginning and an end date. This causes customers to have a sense of urgency and a time limit to purchase.

Questions and Answers – Your customers will have questions about your products and services. Make sure to have answers for them. Take some time and think of the different questions that may be asked and write out your answers. Next, ask a few people to think about other questions that you may have missed. Getting assistance from an outsider will definitely be helpful.

Location – Determine the right location choice for your business type.
Example: office building, mall kiosk, retail store, etc.

Make sure your location is easily accessible to your customers and you have the appropriate permits in place to operate (sign permit, sales tax permit, occupancy permit, etc.). Some business properties will offer yearly lease agreements or month-to-month terms. You will need to ask the property management for specifics.

Lease Agreements Signed (if applicable) – After establishing your business location, you will need to sign a lease agreement, pay first months' rent and possibly a security deposit. Do not forget to negotiate any painting, wall(s) installation or removal, carpet, etc. Once you sign, you are locked in for the duration of the lease term. If you fail to pay on your lease, the property manager can lock your doors until you are caught up; so be sure you budget for your rent expense. Before your lease is up, you can negotiate to renew at the same monthly rate.

 Tip: Start talking about lease renewal and monthly rates well in advance. In the event the monthly rent increases beyond your budget it will give you time to find another more affordable location.

Business Insurance – This is a must have for your business. Do not start your business without proper insurance coverage. Make sure your property, products, and business is covered under your insurance policy. Business owners have ignored this rule and have lost everything.

Sales Tax, EIN, Licensing & Permits – If you are selling products and (some) services to consumers you must have a sales tax permit and pay quarterly sales taxes. Other permits such as an occupancy and sign permit may be required when leasing space and installing a sign. Check with the property manager and/or your local governing authority for exact details.

An EIN will be used if you have employees, to open a business bank account and used on tax filing forms. Also, if certain businesses requests a W-9 (so they can pay you) an EIN/Tax ID number can be used instead of giving out your social security number. EIN is optional for Assumed Names (DBA) and Limited Liability Company (LLC), and required for corporations.

Your business type will determine whether or not you need a license to operate. If you learned your trade in the form of schooling, then the instructor should be able to point you in the right direction for licensing. If you learned your trade from hands-on experience, check with your local governing authority to see if licensing is necessary for you to operate your business.

Software for Customers, Accounting, and Inventory – Make sure you are able to keep up with your customers' information, pay your bills, and track your inventory. Do an Internet search and include your business type to see your available options. Some businesses use an Excel spreadsheet and handwritten checks, so do not spend too much at start-up if it is not necessary. Other businesses will require specialized software so be sure to weigh your options. Remember, some software companies offer software installed on your computer and others offer it in the cloud so you can access your information anywhere with an Internet connection.

Business Equipment – Depending on your business type, you may need more than your standard computer, desk, fax, printer, shelves, and coffee maker to operate your business. Check with several vendors for the absolute best price and quality for your business equipment. If your business equipment is expensive, I suggest leasing the majority of it (if lease option available) until you make the necessary funds to purchase before using financing. By doing it this way, you are able to determine which equipment is absolutely necessary while saving on upfront costs. If you already know the exact equipment you need, and financing is necessary, make sure to shop around for low interest rates.

Employees – Decide which positions are necessary, post hiring ads, and start the interview process. Before making a final decision you might consider background checks, previous employment verification to determine if their previous company would re-hire the applicant, along with high school diploma or college degree verification. Confirm that each employee is trained (if necessary) and knows their responsibilities and job duties.

Hire employees that connect with your company's culture and share some degree of passion towards your business type. If they will be dealing with customers make sure they are likable and enjoy working with people. If they are back-office staff, make sure they are detail and task oriented. You are required to follow the laws set by the US Department of Labor and any state laws your state may have concerning employees.

Payroll – You can use payroll software to help determine wages and taxes. You must make quarterly or monthly employee tax payments and register with your local unemployment office.

Another option (my suggestion) is to hire a payroll company to process it for you, which will save lots of time and paper work.

Unless the type of business you are starting is a payroll company in that case, you should be able to process your own payroll with ease.

Employee Policies & Posters – You are required by law to post certain notices required by our government concerning employees. Those notices can include Minimum Wage Law, Employee Rights, Job Safety (OSHA), Payday Notice, Equal Employment Opportunity, Unemployment Compensation, etc.

Copyrights, Trademarks, & Patents – Before distributing your written, audio, or video work to the public I suggest filing a copyright. Once you are in operation you are able to file a Trademark application for your business name, product name, slogan, design, etc.

If you have an invention and it is not out in the market, then filing a patent on it would be in your best interest.

Refund Policies – Before starting your business you need to determine the circumstances in which you will offer a refund to your customers. Some businesses will offer full refunds while others charge a re-stocking or processing fee. An example would be 10%-20% of the total price. Other companies will issue a refund within a specific time frame while others operate on a strict "no refund" policy.

If you are in the product business and receive the product back and give a refund, you now have a "used" and hopefully undamaged product. You will have to determine if it can be re-sold or you may have to take a loss on the item. If you are a service business "time is money", so you will need to determine at what point you are willing to offer a refund, if any, during the process of fulfilling your services.

There are very fine lines when it comes to giving or not giving refunds. Either way you will lose out on time, money, or both. If you choose to have a "no refund" policy you may end up with several angry customers if they become dissatisfied with your products or services. You are the owner and have the ultimate authority to decide how you want to handle refunds, make your decisions carefully.

Partner or Investor Agreements Signed – If you will be operating with one or more business partners or an investor it is extremely important to go over every detail within your business operation. Each individual should have in writing what they are investing into the business, what they expect to receive in return, their responsibilities, who gets the final say so, etc. Making sure everything is in writing and signed is extremely important before operating your business.

 *Note: If you cannot check off the steps mentioned, go back and make sure that either you complete the step or verify that it is not necessary for your business type. Example: if working from home, a lease agreement does not apply to you.*

Before Opening Day

Advertising Strategy – you will want to market or advertise about 30 days before your grand opening to build anticipation leading up to your opening day. You have possibly seen several companies with a banner stating "Opening Soon" and then change it to "Now Open".

They are informing the public that their products or services will be available soon and are building anticipation.

What to Expect

At this point, you are excited, energized, nervous, and ready to start the day with customers and sales!

Remember, to focus on exceptional customer service and be confident.

On your opening day, you may have customers waiting in line to do business with you. You may only have a handful of customers, or you may have none. Your phone may be ringing off the hook, you may have a few phone calls, or you may have none.

There is no way to know what your customer interaction may be for the very first day. What I can tell you is to **stay focused, stay determined, and always remain positive.**

If your business is not booming with customers on the first day, do not be discouraged. Give it some time and make certain you are energized and remain confident.

If you are a beginner at business, it might be a good thing for there to be only a handful of customers at first. This gives you an opportunity to ensure everything is taken care of correctly and in a timely manner.

Make sure you give the absolute best customer service you can and do not forget to ask for referrals.

In the beginning stages, you might get countless inquiries, which is normal. From time to time, people want to know more about the business before they make a purchase. A lot of consumers make purchases around payday so it may take a few weeks to make sales.

 *Do not forget to ask every satisfied customer to comment or click "like" on your social media pages.*

Welcome

You finally made it to opening day!

If you are here, it is because you have put in the effort and taken the necessary steps to turn your dreams into a reality. I welcome you to the world of entrepreneurship. There will be challenging and rewarding days ahead, this is just the beginning.

READY · SET · SELL!!!!

Chapter 32

New Small Businesses

"Keep focused, deliver outstanding customer service, and don't forget to ask for referrals!"

At this point, your business is open and fully operational.

Your **"Now Open"** sign or website is up and you are open for business.

Placing ads, answering inquiries, and customer service are your normal routines. Your plan and strategy is in place and your main goals are gaining new customers and retaining your existing ones.

You should be filled with energy and excitement and telling everyone you come across about the products and services you offer. Business cards should be given out to potential customers and asking for referrals is a common practice.

Some businesses will flourish very quickly and others take some time to obtain a steady flow of customers. Advertising or face-to-face marketing will help ensure that your products and services are being viewed by potential customers.

Having customers take the next step and purchase from you will depend upon;

- Your advertising message and how it connected with your target market.

- Your price and the quality of your products or services.

- Whether your products or services are in demand at that time.

- How you present your business, yourself, and your products and services.

- Your ability to provide your products or services in a timely manner to meet customer demand.

- If your hours of operation are aligned with the hours your customers are able to purchase from you.

- If you provided multiple methods for customers to use when purchasing from you. Example: over the phone, online, in person, etc.

Every single day consumers or other businesses are purchasing either products or services they need or want. The question is who are they purchasing from; your business or your competition. Give them several reasons to choose your business and to keep coming back.

Not Experiencing the Customers You Expected?

Be patient, continue to advertise, present your products and services with passion and excellence. Have a genuine desire to provide a product or service that will increase the satisfaction of your customers.

Remember, just because you think you have the absolute best products or services and everyone should purchase them right away; does not mean that everyone agrees with you. You are a new business and people may need to get familiar with seeing your ads and learning more about the products and services you offer before deciding to purchase from you.

It may take a while to pinpoint the best way for your business to operate and generate sales. Your business may be doing all the right things it just may be taking longer to get going.

My business is not making many sales, what can I do about it?

This is a tough question to answer because there are many different factors and business types. Here are some common reasons why sales slowdown or come to a halt and examples of what you can do about it.

1. **No advertising or face-to-face marketing.** You can not solely rely on telling your relatives and friends about your new business. Start advertising and marketing face-to-face immediately. When marketing face-to-face, do not just focus and talk about your products and services. Engage the consumer with small talk; learn a little about the consumer or business you are communicating with. Develop a mutual conversation then add your products and services into it.

2. **Advertising methods are not reaching your target market (potential customers).** Ensure the advertising method you are using is reaching your potential customers. The company you are advertising through (ex. Print Ad Company) should be able to provide you with a detailed list of the people who most likely viewed their advertisements. If your ads are still not working after verifying, possibly consider changing your ad or using another advertising method.

3. **Your advertising messages are not clear or not communicating effectively.** Ask around and verify that your message is clear and understandable. Make sure they are speaking to your potential audience in a way they can relate to and understand.

4. **Prices are too high and customers cannot afford what you offer.** Possibly lower your prices and offer discounts to new or repeat customers. Another option to consider is offering credit terms through a financing company. Conduct research to verify if your type of business qualifies for finance companies to offer credit terms to your customers. This will allow your customers to make payments instead of paying everything up front. You will be paid from the finance company in full and your customers will make monthly payments to the finance company.

5. **Do you have a referral program to reward customers for referring clients to you?** In the beginning stages of your business, your main goal should be making sales but how will you make those sales if consumers or other businesses do not know your business exists? Consider offering a referral program and reward customers for referring others to you. Rewards can be discounts for future purchases or a percentage of the total sale.

6. **Are you offering your products and services in person, over the phone, through the mail, and online?** Having multiple ways for customers to purchase from you is ideal, especially if not all of your customers can visit your location.

7. **Your website is not being viewed and/or what you offer is not clear.** You need to make sure your business information along with your website is registered on as many search engines as possible. If your budget allows, start "pay per click" ads on search engines that your customers are likely to use. If you are familiar with blogging then start one for your business. On social media, make sure you are including your website name on your posts. Have a few people review your website to determine if what you have on there is clear and easy to understand.

8. **Hours of operation.** Your business hours should be the hours your customers are most likely to purchase from you. If not then you could be losing valuable sales to your competitors.

9. **Your products or services are not in high or medium demand at this time.** Depending on what products or services you offer, there could be a low demand for them at this time. Do some research and find out if there is a peak season for your products and services to sell. Example: some toy stores flourish during the Christmas holidays and the tourist industry is in high demand during the summer months.

10. **Competition. Do you constantly have to compete with other companies in the same field?** Are you located near them? Are their prices lower than yours? In every industry, there are large, medium, and small businesses. In some cases, it is almost impossible to beat large companies on price and advertising campaigns. However, if you constantly let your customers know that you can offer "one on one" personal assistance, it might be what helps them decide to purchase from you.

11. **Do it yourself.** Make a determination if your products and services are something that most consumers can simply make or do themselves. Make sure there is a value placed on your products or services and promote your expertise and experience in your field.

12. **Customer Service.** Make sure you and your employees are offering the absolute best customer services possible. Do not take on too much that it causes your customers to feel like you are ignoring them or they are not important to you.

13. **Slow response time.** If you are the only one working on your business, you have to take on several additional duties other than working directly with customers.

Consider hiring commissioned sales reps to handle sales while you handle customer service, processing, and other duties specific to your business.

14. **Accountability.** Give your customers assurance that you are credible by letting them know the years of experience in your field and promote testimonies from previous customers. Stay accountable to your customers, answer their calls, and their emails in a timely manner. If you are not able to that, then you may consider hiring help before taking on additional customers.

15. **Are you positioned in an environment where your customers can find you?** Make certain your location is accessible and easy to find. If you are an online company, ensure that your website is getting the exposure necessary to attract new clients.

Why are similar businesses experiencing success and mine is not?

This is an extremely difficult question to answer without knowing exact details of your business type, plan, strategy, sales script, etc. However, I can advise you to carefully consider these possible facts about similar businesses.

1. They may have been established years ago and over time have developed a large and faithful customer base.

2. Their prices may be more favorable when considering your target market. Make sure to research multiple suppliers who may be able to give you better deals, you can then pass those savings on to your customers. You may also consider price matching your competition, this refers to matching the prices of your competitions advertised price for their products or services.

3. They may have a more aggressive sales tactic approach.

4. They may be reaching out to a different target market than you are and obtaining more customers. Do your research beforehand and know exactly who your target market is and where they are most likely to view your advertisements.

5. Their budget could be very high which allows them to advertise significantly more than their competitors.

6. Some businesses choose dishonest tactics to win customers, which is not suggested.

It is hard to see similar businesses flourishing when yours is not. At some point many business owners have experienced that feeling. Very famous and successful business owners at one point started somewhere and faced challenges similar to what you may be facing. What separates them is the fact that they never gave up. They kept pushing forward, kept changing what needed adjusting and held on until things flourished.

I encourage you to look at your business plan and strategy and see if anything needs changing then move forward with confidence. Next, look at what similar businesses are doing and compare your strategy with theirs. What are the differences and similarities? Are they advertising more, offering lower prices, have stronger guarantees, etc.?

Do not be discouraged; change what needs changing, re-position your business strategy if necessary and stay focused.

Are you experiencing a steady or great amount of customers?

You are on the right track!

Keep focused, deliver outstanding customer service, ask for referrals, and keep doing what you are doing.

Conceive new ways to improve your existing performance, to make it better, faster, and more convenient. If you need to hire staff to help you efficiently service your customers; now is the time. You want to assure all your customers are receiving the attention they must have to make their experience *exceptional*. Customer referrals are an added avenue to increase your sales.

To save and utilize your valuable time, I suggest using a payroll company. This will allow you to focus on your company and not payroll taxes or additional paperwork.

Focus on Your Business Process

In the beginning stages of developing your business, focus on your business processes before immediate expansion.

Business Process– make sure your operations are flowing properly, your costs are low, and you have a steadily increasing cash flow along with a savings plan. Also, make certain your advertising and sales methods are working by attracting new customers and retaining existing ones before deciding to add new products or services (optional), expand, or open more locations.

> **Add new products or services** – Waiting is optional, if the new product or service will not disrupt your cash flow or if your customers prepay, then adding new products or services is fine as long as you are certain they will sell.
>
> **Expand** – Add more office or warehouse space to your existing operations.
>
> **Open More Locations**– Establishing multiple business units.
>
> **Savings** – It is highly suggested you have a minimum of 6 months of your operational expenses in a savings or investment account.

After you have your business process in order, begin thinking of expansion; position yourself to take the necessary steps to move forward. Keep costs low and be certain every risk is worth it. Take risks a fraction at a time, meaning slowly, take three steps forward then one-step back to confirm you are moving forward and in the right direction.

Know Which Advertisements Work

Ensure that you have a clear-cut idea of which advertisement strategies are working for you.

It is very important that you do not try too many different advertising methods at once, unless you are tracking how every customer heard about you.

Many customers state they heard about your business online. Was it the result of an Internet search or an online ad? Other customers may state they were told about your business from a family member or friend. How did that family member or friend hear about your business? They may or may not know. Accurate record keeping is imperative to learning how customers found out about your business. It is extremely important to know which advertising campaign works: keeping you from throwing away your money on methods that do not work.

Trial and Error

As a new business owner you may have to try out different strategies until you find what best works for your business.

Those different strategies include:

- Advertising Methods.

- Advertising Message.

- Sales Scripts.

- Sales Approach.

- Pricing & Presentation.

- Hours of Operation.

- Policies and Refunds.

- And Many More Depending on Your Business Type.

It may take trial and error to find which strategy fits your business type, attracts the most customers, and delivers the best customer satisfaction. Do not spend too much of your cash flow while in the process of trial and error and trying different strategies.

Once you find which strategy works best then focus on that while continuing to keep costs low.

Be Willing to Change or Adjust

During the process of operating your business the need for changes or adjustments may arise. Whether with your process, your staff, or the way you handle customers, equipment, shipping, etc. It is common for a business owner to learn something one way and keep it the same forever. However, if you study very successful businesses, you will find that most have gone through changes and adjustments.

- Businesses went from mailing documents to faxing them now emailing them.

- Businesses used to require actual ink signatures and now for some electronic signatures will do.

- Certain processes used to take months and now can be handled in a few days with advanced equipment and new procedures.

- Ultrasounds can now be taken at very early stages of pregnancy.

- Cellular phones went from only being used for calling purposes to the now smart phones which are like mini computers in your pocket.

As times change, technology advances, or new developments occur; be willing to change, adjust, or let go of old ways and develop new and more cost effective alternatives.

Only make cautious and necessary changes or adjustments that will benefit your customers and your business.

Chapter 33

Give Back

There are so many places in the world that lack the basic necessities of life; the ones we take for granted daily.

As your business grows, I suggest you take part in lending a helping hand to an organization focused on providing necessities to those who do not possess them. You can do so by helping support various organizations monetarily or actually take part in the helping process by volunteering your time. I have found that a first-hand experience is the best way to understand the need and recognize how you can make a difference.

Helping the less fortunate in the US or abroad is a personal decision. Thus, I will not offer any suggestions as to an organization or country. If you feel the desire to help, pick a category, then choose where you want to help. Do an Internet search and find the organizations that are working in that area. Confirm their reputation, status, and testimonies before donating.

Your donations should be 100% tax deductible if the organization has a main office in the US.

Examples of types of donations could be:

- School supplies for children in need.

- Providing food, clothing, or bill assistance to less fortunate families.

- Helping build homes for homeless families.

- Donating to inner city youth programs.

- Relief from natural disasters.

- Military organizations that assist veterans.

- After school art or music programs.

- Animal shelters.

- Plus many more.

If you choose to support, be sure to let your customers know what projects you are donating to. In doing so, they can feel that they are a part of something rewarding.

Here is a sample text you can display to your customers.

"Every time you purchase from us 5% of the proceeds goes toward feeding homeless children in Africa. Thank you, without your support this would not be possible."

Your customers may appreciate your donations going to a good cause and choose to participate as well.

Chapter 34

Thank You

Thank you so much for taking the time to read this instructional handbook. It has truly been an honor to serve you and to give you guidance on starting your new business venture or continuing with your existing one.

My sincere hope is that this instructional handbook has given you the insight, answers, and options you need in starting and/or operating your small business.

Earlier in this book, I asked you, "what success was to you." I pray that your answer to that question will be a daily reality in your life. Remember, every day we can either step forward or backward, towards or away from our goals. You may not be where you want to be in life but that does not mean it has to stay that way. Sometimes doors of opportunity open in our lives and then there are times we have to open them ourselves.

You will never go further than what you can believe, so believe BIG!.

Business is like life, there are ups and downs. Be grateful when up and stay positive when down.

The Small Business Assistance of America staff has worked countless hours to complete this project. Knowing that our labor will help you in your endeavors has made it well worth the effort.

Register your email address on our website www.SmallBusinessAA.com to receive updates, advice, tips, encouragement, new product releases and exclusive content.

Finally, I encourage you to find other resources that will give you further guidance when necessary.

Never stop learning and increasing knowledge.

Remember, stay focused, never give up, take positive steps and always move forward.

Thank you,

Henry G. Solomon
Small Business Consultant

Bibliography

Cited References & Resources

Frank Wikipedia. *"http://www.freeinfosociety.com/site.php?postnum=808."* n.d. *http://www. freeinfosociety.com/.* February 2014.

Doyle, Allison *http://jobsearch.about.com/od/jobsearchglossary/g/glossary-definition.html/.* 14 December 2013. 2013.

Administration, Small Business. *www.sba.gov.* 23 February 2014.

Advocacy, SBA Office of. *http://www.sba.gov/sites/default/files/FAQ_March_2014_0.pdf.* 03 2014. FAQ. 28 March 2014.

AT&T. *http://www.corp.att.com/history/history1.html.* 20 March 2014.

Backley, Steve. *http://www.goodreads.com/author/show/5763924.Steve_Backley.* Original Quote. 10 April 2014.

Bezos, Jeffrey Preston. *http://www.biography.com/people/jeff-bezos-9542209.* 10 April 2014.

Bing. *http://www.bing.com/search?q=definition+of+administration&src=IE-TopResult&FORM=IE1 1TR&conversationid=. Powered by Oxford Dictionary.* 28 April 2014.

BizLaw.about.com.

> Business Property Tax.
> *http://biztaxlaw.about.com/od/typesofbusinesstaxes/a/propertytax.htm.* 28 May 2014.

> Personal Property Tax.
> *http://biztaxlaw.about.com/od/glossaryp/g/personalprop.htm.* 28 May 2014.

> Franchise Tax.
> *http://biztaxlaw.about.com/od/glossaryf/g/franchisetax.htm.* 28 May 2014.

Business Dictionary.

    Marketing.
    http://www.businessdictionary.com/definition/marketing.html. 10 April 2014.

    Mission Statement.
    http://http://www.businessdictionary.com/definition/mission-statement.html. 10 April 2014.

    Work Environment
    http://www.businessdictionary.com/definition/work-environment.html. 20 December 2013.

Census. *http://www.census.gov/eos/www/naics/.* 21 June 2014.

Davidson Sr., Arthur. *http://www.biography.com/people/arthur-davidson-21008533.* 15 Mar 2014.

Dell, Michael. *http://www.biography.com/people/michael-dell-9542199.* 15 March 2014.

Dictionary.

    Budget.
    http://dictionary.reference.com/browse/positive. 11 December 2013.

    Partner.
    http://dictionary.reference.com/browse/partner 28 April 2014.

    Positive.
    http://dictionary.reference.com/browse/positive. 12 December 2013.

    Trademark
    http://dictionary.reference.com/browse/trademark?s=t. 22 June 2014

    Copyright.
    http://dictionary.reference.com/browse/copyright?s=t. 30 June 2014

    Invent.
    http://dictionary.reference.com/browse/invent?s=t. 12 September 2014

    Invention.
    http://dictionary.reference.com/browse/invention?s=t. 13 April 2014

Patent.

http://dictionary.reference.com/browse/patent?s=t. 7 March 2014

Disney, Walter Elias. *http://www.biography.com/people/walt-disney-9275533.* 15 March 2014.

Edison, Thomas A. "WWW.brainyquote.com/quotes/authors/t/thomas_a_edison.html." n.d. *Brainy Quote.* 2013.

Google.

    Ethics.
    https://www.google.com/#q=definition+of+ethics. 15 September 2014.

    Expectations.
    https://www.google.com/#q=definition+of+expectations. 24 March 2014.

    Goals.
    https://www.google.com/#q=definition+of+goals. 14 April 2014.

    Accounting.
    https://www.google.com/#q=what+is+accounting. 2 August 2014.

    Values.
    https://www.google.com/#q=definition+of+values. 9 July 2014.

Harley, William Sylvester. *http://www.biography.com/people/william-s-harley-20903181.* 15 March 2014.

Investopedia.

    Brand Identity.
    http://www.investopedia.com/terms/b/brand-identity.asp. 16 May 2014.

    Federal Income Tax.
    http://www.investopedia.com/terms/f/federal_income_tax.asp. 8 May 2014.

    EIN.
    http://www.investopedia.com/terms/e/employer-identification-number.asp. 24 February 2014.

    Marketing.
    http://www.investopedia.com/terms/m/marketing.asp. 10 April 2014.

    Medicare Tax
    http://www.investopedia.com/terms/m/medicarewages.asp. 14 June 2014.

egotiation.
http://www.investopedia.com/terms/n/negotiation.asp. 12 June 2014.

Sales Ta.
http://www.investopedia.com/terms/s/salestax.asp. 22 July 2014.

Social Security Ta.
http://www.investopedia.com/terms/s/social-security-tax.asp. 2 May 2014.

Jobs, Steven Paul. http://www.biography.com/people/steve-jobs-9354805. 15 March 2014.

ogos. *http://www.famouslogos.org/logos/nike-logo.* 24 February 2014.

Luisa Kroll and Kerry A. Dolan. "http://www.forbes.com/profile/arthur-blank/." March
2014. *http://www.forbes.com/.* February 2014.

Macy's. *http://www.macysinc.com/press-room/logo-photo-gallery/default.aspx.* 03 March 2014.

Page, arry. *http://www.biography.com/people/larry-page-12103347.* 15 March 2014.

Penney, J. C. "http://www.borgraphy.com/people/jcpenney-38638." 2014. *The Biography
Channel website.* 06 March 2014.

Sanders, Colonel Harland. "http://www.kfc.com/images/pdf/COLONELS_JOURNEY_Full_
Eng.pdf." 2012. *http://colonelsanders.com/.* February 2014.

SBA, eneral Small Business oans.
https://www.sba.gov/content/7a-loan-program-eligibility. 20 December 2014.

YourDicionary, n.d. Web.

http://examples.yourdictionary.com/examples/examples-of-core-values.html. n.d. *10 March
2014.*

http://www.yourdictionary.com/certificate-of-occupancy#law. 12 January 2014

Merriam-Webster, n.d. Web. *http://Merriam-Webster.com/dictionary/sale>.
Merriam-Webster, 2014.Web. 8 May 2014.*